The Book Of The
Heavy Horse

A guide to every aspect of the heavy horse world
which will delight all those who admire these
majestic creatures.

The Book Of The
Heavy Horse

EDWARD HART

Patrick Stephens, Wellingborough

First published 1986

British Library Cataloguing in Publication Data
Hart, Edward
The book of the heavy horse.
1. Draft horses
I. Title
636.1'4   SF311

ISBN 0-85059-648-0

Patrick Stephens Limited is part of the
Thorsons Publishing Group

Text photoset in 10 on 11 pt Goudy Old Style
by Avocet Marketing Services, Aylesbury, Bucks.
Printed in Great Britain on 115 gsm Fineblade coated cartridge,
and bound, by the Garden City Press, Letchworth, Herts,
for the publishers, Patrick Stephens Limited,
Denington Estate, Wellingborough, Northants,
NN8 2QD, England.

Contents

Introduction

The world's heavy horse breeds stand apart. Their main function is to pull a heavy load at the walk and, whereas the various riding disciplines are inter-linked, the big horses have much less in common with any other equine class.

Britain has four main breeds of heavy horse: Clydesdale, Percheron, Shire and Suffolk. North America provides a fifth in the American Belgian, a quite different animal from its European ancestor. The Continent has a whole list of breeds which will be discussed later in the book.

The horse's history as a draught animal is comparatively short. Until the late 18th and early 19th centuries oxen provided the main pulling power. Not until the early to mid-19th century when lighter ploughs and a new range of farm machines were developed did the heavy horse become really widespread.

When the population and popularity of the heavy horse seemed boundless, along came mechanisation and the motor. Churchill observed that the replacement of the horse by the internal combustion engine marked a gloomy chapter in the progress of mankind.

Harking back to the old days. Bullock waggon in the American style (Eustis).

Cart horse type c 1800.

As the demise of the heavy horse began in about 1950, its period of supremacy was little more than a century. Yet what a surge of development took place in that time, and what a legacy and legend has been bequeathed us! The horse's influence was all pervading; men's whole lives were devoted to breeding, training, selling or working the heavy horse breeds.

A postcard from c 1900 showing the Christmas dole being delivered on the Chatsworth Estate.

A splendid type of work horse stallion, name unknown. The period is probably Edwardian judging from the enthusiastic groom's dress (Angela Mulliner).

FASCINATION

I noticed as a boy, spending much time among horsemen, that those who were most skilled with the big horses often had little interest in any other sort. Frequently they could not ride, apart from sitting side-saddle on a swaying Suffolk back as it walked to and from the fields. Ponies, race horses, steeplechasers and hunters were as another species.

Fortunately the converse is not true, for all 'horsey' people seem to have a soft spot for the heavies. At Wembley's Horse of the Year show each October, no event is more popular than the March of the Heavy Horses, weaving their intricate patterns in the sand as their harrows clink within inches of each other, and the whole arena rises to them.

Even when heavy horses were part of the everyday scene, some artists and writers loved them above all others. Today, when so much power may be tapped by pressing a button or turning an ignition key, the Suffolk or Percheron attracts through contrast. You can see the mighty muscles working, sense the strain as the horse leans into its collar, look up to the great head and feel the vibration as the iron-shod hoof strikes road or sod for a grip.

THE GENTLE GIANT

In general the heavy breeds are more phlegmatic than others. They bear little relation to the more highly strung Arab or Thoroughbred, ready to prance or 'spook' at the slightest excuse. For this reason the heavies are sometimes termed 'the gentle giants', but the title may be misleading. Most heavy horses are quiet, but individual exceptions can prove dangerous if too many liberties are taken with them. If in a row of Suffolks at a major show there is one loose box faced by a metal grid, leave it well alone, and concentrate your affections on the friendly heads leaning over the half-doors.

It is not part of a big horse's nature to tread on your foot deliberately, but an accidental occurrence can result in real damage. So keep your distance; the professional horsemen and women turn their charges with arm extended, and body leaning away, minimising the chance of a ton descending on their boot.

There were, and are, rogue horses. Most are man-made, through ill-usage, and the real 'wrong-uns' have generally been culled, though not always before their genes were passed on to perpetuate the faults. Horses not in regular work are more likely to be upset by crowds than those that are, and the crowds themselves are less familiar with the likely reactions of big animals. 'Care at all stages' is the watchword.

WORKING

The show ground's undoubted glamour, where the country's top horses assemble with brasses shining and plumes tossing, is one world. Field and forest form another, for some of our keenest horsemen have little interest in showing, but much for using horse power to cultivate the land and to harvest its fruits. For such people there is a special pleasure in working a team so that all pull together, the horses responding to a familiar voice and scarcely needing the reins leading from their mouths to the horseman's hands.

'Ploughing with horses is work in its most pleasantly disguised form' said a farmer in the 1930s. Today the chance to harrow behind a pair of Shires has become part and parcel of Heavy Horse Workings, those 'fun' weekends open to everyone. For the ploughman and his (or her) team have no need of those transistor radios fitted to modern tractor cabs to obviate boredom, no cause to

Mr Barry Coffen's Clydesdale geldings ploughing at Wokingham, Berkshire. Note that the horses are joined by a coupling rein, and that each is tied back to the other's collar (Colin Fry).

wear ear plugs to drown the din. The horseman hears the birds singing in the hedgerows every time he reaches the headland; his horses are his companions, and like the hill shepherd with his dogs, he is never lonely, though far from human kind.

Though all heavy horses are bred and reared on farms and in fields, many spend part of their lives on city streets. In the horse's heyday this was the basis of a regular industry. The youngster grew up in a shady pasture with its dam, was weaned among a party of fellow striplings, and fed well summer and winter until about three years old. Then came the day of training, or 'breaking' in the horseman's rather inapt terminology. Harrows and plough were followed by the more demanding cart or waggon, and at five years old the mature animal could be sold and warranted 'quiet in all gears'. Life changed. From muddy November track at the end of a day's ploughing, a less varying regime was entered, hauling a delivery dray or a coal rulley, alone or as one of a pair.

Cheap and apparently limitless fuel ended the heavy horse's role on the streets. Threats of petrol shortages, steep rises in its price and that of insurance, plus the slow rate of modern city traffic through its mass use, have again brought the horse into the reckoning as a source of power. Some of the forecast difficulties, such as workers' unwillingness to care for stabled horses seven days a week, have not materialised. The brewery horsemen, to the fore in this line, are as ardent in their care for the big horses as were their counterparts on the land. No one who has poured a skepful of oats and chaff into a manger under a Shire's muzzle, or bedded down a stomping Suffolk last thing on a winter's night, ever really forgets. This book tells the story of the big horses in every detail.

Chain harrowing grassland with a Percheron mare in Surrey. The owner/driver is Nick Hayyez (Colin Fry).

Chapter 1
Back from the brink

The heavy horse's revival is one of the most astounding phenomena in the long history of man's relationship with animals. The cart horse became apparently outmoded; its very name was associated with plodding and dullness. The internal combustion engine appeared set to condemn the heavy horse to obscurity if not extinction. That it did not becomes apparent in these pages. The story is one of grit and determination, a literal 'never say die' spirit among a small company of breeders who kept faith with their animals when all seemed stacked against them.

Like many great victories, the heavy horse's survival was won against huge odds and by the narrowest of margins. In the 20 years between 1950 and 1970, very few foals were being bred. For part of that dreary time, only two journalists were present at the National Heavy Horse Show at Peterborough, which then covered both Shires and Percherons. One of them was my predecessor on *Horse & Hound*, the late Andy Wyndham-Brown, a writer of colossal experience with all types of horses. The farming Press had lost interest, working horses were not 'with it'. They drew no advertising, and so what little hold they had in farming minds was stifled. Oil was cheap and apparently limitless, machinery easy to secure on hire purchase at a low bank rate. No one operated a hire purchase service for horses.

Their few owners had little need anyway. Those horses remaining on farms were kept mainly for personal reasons. 'Blossom and Beauty were foaled in the year we came here. They shall see their time out.' 'Old Tom will be miserable if we get rid of Patch and Bonny. They might as well stay till he retires. They can lead a few turnips out in winter and drill the mangels.' 'These horses were slaves when I was a slave, so they shall retire here.' Such were typical reasons for the few heavy horses that remained on British farms during the 1950s and 1960s. The old stagers hung on, but were seldom replaced. Foals became a rarity.

But what is spring without a foal in the home paddock? Pony numbers grew, so blacksmiths stayed in business through attending to the children's steeds, or by turning to welding or wrought ironwork. Whatever the means, it is fortunate for us that the smiths did survive.

A regular outlet had existed for farm geldings, but this vanished with the motor van and the heavy lorry, the light shunting engine and hydraulic power. Only one market remained. To their great credit, the horse-owning breweries retained their teams, partly for their advertising value and partly because of their suitability for

A pair of Cleveland Bays from Scottish and Newcastle Breweries. This breed was formerly used for farm work in north east Yorkshire but were then rather heavier (Gavin Cole).

short hauls. I suspect that some company chairmen did not want to see their highly skilled and professional horsemen forced into a way of life for which they had neither liking nor aptitude, and that the balance sheets of the time could stand that indulgence. Any decent male horses were gelded in the hope of a brewery sale, resulting in a shortage of quality stallions. This made an acute situation even worse, and all the time the machine was gaining ground, with new mechanical devices by the hundred yearly.

During this period North America, cradle of the internal combustion engine, was showing a revival of interest in literal horse power. Prairie farms had abandoned their teams in the 1920s and '30s, before the great decline in Britain. In Canada and the USA during the 1960s interest in the horse was slowly awakening, yet there too the draught horse population had declined to the point where the new band of enthusiasts could not find the sort they wanted.

Arlin Wareing, son of a Shire man, came to Britain on a preliminary survey in 1969. He returned to interest Maurice Telleen, whose *Draft Horse Journal* is a potent force in keeping the American heavy horse world in being and moving. These two organised a party of 45 who visited Britain in 1970, attended the National Heavy Horse Show, looked at the leading studs, travelled England's green and pleasant land and generally had the time of their lives. They liked what

Vaux Brewery Percherons taking the obstacle course at Beamish Horse Driving Trials, County Durham, 1982 (Gavin Cole).

they saw, and bought some that they liked. They promised future orders. They spread a spirit of optimism among British breeders that had been absent for 30 years.

Maurice Telleen gave a graphic account of the tour in *Draft Horse Journal*, May 1970. He called it 'The Incredible Journey' and defined 'incredible' as 'seeming too unusual or improbable to be possible':

The group hailed from 11 states and one Canadian province. They represented Belgian, Clydesdale, Percheron and Shire horses. They came back with eight more horses; four Suffolks, two Shires and two Percherons.

On a bright and beautiful London day the first stop was at Young & Co's Ram Brewery. And literally the first sight on alighting from the coach was six splendid black Shire geldings. The company keeps 22 working geldings, only three less than 35 years ago. They do three journeys a day within a three mile radius, delivering 10,000 tons of beer a year.

The following forenoon a similar visit was made to Mann, Crossman & Paulin's Brewery, and again the horses and hospitality were superb, with Mr Anthony Crossman, President of the Shire Horse Society, doing the honours.

On Easter Sunday morning we left for Whitbread & Co's Brewery and another inspection of the Shires that deliver London's beer. Here Mr Ruocco, the Stable Manager, was a most congenial and informative host.

From our group 15 volunteers became part of the Easter Parade in London's Battersea Park. They rode on a dray pulled by four of Young's black Shires.

Monday morning saw us off bright and early to a section of England known as East Anglia. An area without wild moors, humming industrial cities and great sea ports, it is flat, low-lying land devoted mainly to agriculture. From here have sprung some of our most honoured and useful breeds of livestock, among them the Suffolk draft horse.

The party's visit chanced to coincide with the Suffolk Horse Society's centennial show, with 20 entries. It was not always thus; the record was in 1921, with 99 head, and even in 1944 Suffolk entries totalled 94. The late secretary W. J. Woods looked after the party, and Maurice Telleen's summing-up has been proven: 'The breeders that remain are a determined and dedicated lot who intend to assure the future of the breed.'

From there the tourists met Mr Morbey of Stuntney for lunch at the Cutter's Inn. Their host has carried out his promise to continue breeding Shires under Cole Ambrose Ltd and the Stuntney prefix: 'That evening we were guests of the Shire and Percheron Societies at a banquet, which surely rates as the social highlight of the tour', continued Maurice Telleen. 'It had all the earmarks of the careful planning and preparation of Roy Bird, the very able and energetic Shire Secretary. The seating arrangements were such that Americans and English were thoroughly mixed — as it should be at events of this type. This memorable night was presided over by Mr Crossman, and climaxed by bringing two Shires into the ballroom.' Next day the party saw the National Heavy Show at Peterborough, then split up into individual forays. What happened next typifies the heavy horse world.

A number of members visited the Trumans, an East Anglian family, some of whom last century left their native March in East Anglia for the USA. They set up as pioneer Shire importers, and were responsible for many hundreds of stallions crossing the Atlantic. Others visited Mr and Mrs J. B. Cooke, who had sold them Jim's Chieftain as a two-year-old stallion two years previously. Much of the present success of the American Shire derives from Jim's Chieftain. This intertwining of past and present is found throughout our story. One human lifetime is little enough in which to really improve a slowly reproducing animal like the horse. And one country can do better when it has others with whom to exchange ideas and blood. Percherons were not neglected, and Mr G. E. Sneath's Pinchbeck stud was raided, two mares being bought.

The party re-formed and headed north, taking in Sunderland in County Durham and seeing the Vaux stables. Percherons were again to the fore here, with Major Wilson as host. Several of the singles, pairs and fours harnessed were bred at Pinchbeck.

Visitor Dave Haxton of Ohio had attended the Scotstoun Stallion Show in 1911 as a 17-year-old! This show is staged in urban Glasgow, and is the site of the male Cawdor Cup championship. The female blue ribande is awarded at the

Royal Highland Show each June, but long before that date the 45 happy North Americans had returned home with stories enough for a lifetime.

As the 1970s progressed, oil prices rose, and supplies were periodically threatened. Tractor prices shot up from £200 for an 'Old Fordson' during World War 2, and under £500 for a 20 hp Ferguson in the early 1950s, to £15,000 for a

Below *A smart pair of Shires driven by Fred Harlock of Thorney, Peterborough at the Walkington Hayride, East Riding, 1982 (Gavin Cole).*

Bottom *Modern use of the horse as an advertising agent.*

sophisticated monster by 1980. Combine harvesters were held inside factories by strikers just as the corn was ripe, and in general the miracle of the machine had lost much gloss.

Slowly, people began talking about horses for draught once more. Where once a Rolls Royce had been a status symbol, the fashion changed to horse power for a wedding, moving house, opening a new store or launching a product. Heavy horses were the antidote to mechanical tedium. People looked at them, when a score of new cars did not gain a second glance. They became a film maker's delight, both for contemporary and period work. To meet the demand, heavy horse centres appeared.

Left *Shires in the harvest field. Corn being led at Hasholme Carr Farm, Yorkshire (Gavin Cole).*

Top right *Six horses with cultivator, driven by Andrew Morton. Note that only two reins are used, attached to the outside bit rings of the lead horses (Gavin Cole).*

Right *Enthusiasts can now drive the big horses at Open Days. Harrowing with Suffolks (Audrey Hart).*

Below *A typical working Shire mare resting after a hard day's work (Gavin Cole).*

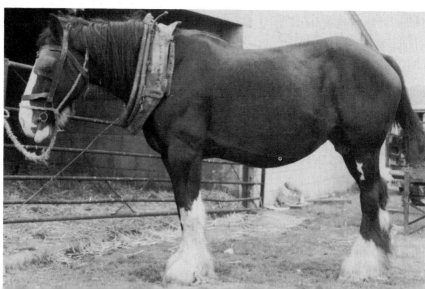

Geoff Morton at Hasholme Carr Farm, Holme upon Spalding Moor, East Riding of Yorkshire, continued through thick and thin to work his 120 acres with horses. Photographers, starved of heavies for 30 years, found them immeasurably photogenic. So many approached Geoff Morton that they became an embarrassment to his work, yet the good-natured Yorkshireman did not wish to turn any away.

He solved the problem by opening his farm to the public on specific weekends; in spring at seedtime and during harvest time in autumn. A small charge was made, giving visitors freedom of the acres. They snapped a Saddleback sow suckling 11 noisy piglets, took sound recordings of horses' hooves approaching, committed to film the straight furrows or eight-horse team, had rides on a waggon and even drove a steady horse in the harrows.

With all this publicity, Geoff Morton found that he had to keep twice as many horses as the farm required for normal work. Some would be away filming, or

conducting a bride to church, with another team in Market Weighton or Hull to promote consumer goods. The heavy horse was finding a new niche in the modern world of the late 20th century, and Hasholme Carr is now open more frequently.

Other heavy horse centres sprang up. Courage opened their new stables at Maidenhead by inviting all Shire Horse Society members. Expecting a hundred or two, their organisational powers were stretched by the convergence of apparently every member of the Society on the Courage Shire Horse Centre! By 1984 the Centre was attracting 140,000 visitors each summer. Such colossal interest was also tapped by the Devon Shire Horse Centre at Yealmpton, Plymouth. Before long it gained a Tourist Board Award, and gives pleasure to thousands each year.

The straining sinews of the Shire and Clydesdale teams strike an atavistic chord in the spectators. Accustomed to power at the turn of a switch, they are fascinated to see it in living things, awed by the majestic height of the great geldings, or enraptured by the big foals gambolling in the shade or lying flat out asleep in the summer sun.

In response to this demand harness makers once again catered for the big ones; farriers made large shoes alongside the hunters' and ponies'. Cart and waggon restorers found they had more work than they could cope with.

At last the chicken-and-egg situation was broken. The heavy horse's resurgence was delayed because there was not enough good harness, or anything to pull.

Left *Geldings owned by Mr David Bowyer, Berkshire and driven by Mr Jack Read and Terry Toon drilling corn in Windsor Park. A dead straight line is the aim, obtained by running the drill wheel in the previous wheeling* (Colin Fry).

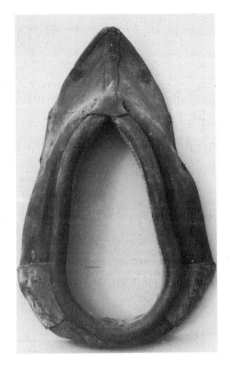

Right *A much-patched and worn collar* (Gavin Cole).

Craftsmen and suppliers did not risk setting up in the heavy horse business because they had no idea of the scope of the market. So materials 40 years old, weakened and out-dated, had to be used.

Another breakthrough came in the late 1970s when Charles Pinney began to manufacture horse-drawn implements using modern materials. A wooden cart looks splendid in the show ring, but for crop spraying or fertiliser spreading it is better and cheaper to use glass fibre and other synthetics. Demand is growing at home and overseas, for governments are at last seeing that the small power unit which keeps people on the land is infinitely preferable to complex systems that throw them on the unemployed heap in cities.

Charles Pinney reports growing enquiries from a wide range of farmers. Almost all modern machinery is designed to operate under more favourable conditions than the steep and inaccessible hillsides which are being improved as more and more sound lowland is taken by builders. Horses have considerable natural stability, and a tractive power in wet conditions that puts the most sophisticated all-terrain vehicle to shame. Horses can prepare seedbeds, sow pastures and harvest them in conditions where it would be dangerous to use a conventional tractor. Horse mowers have a low centre of gravity, so they may be used to cut grass, weeds or bracken on quite steep banks.

A sledge is even more useful than a cart in very hilly districts. A surprising number of hay bales may be loaded and fed to outlying cattle, and the sledge cuts

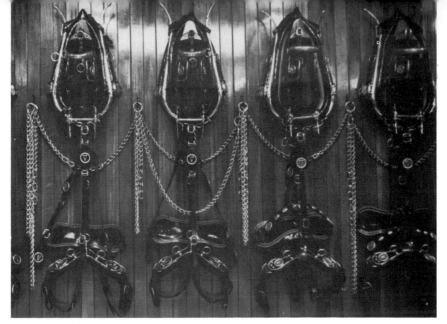

Above *Show harness in Vaux Brewery's stables at Sunderland (Gavin Cole).*

Left *Old saddles at a farm sale (Gavin Cole).*

Above right *Dutch barge harness.*

Below *Selling cart harness at York Livestock .Centre in 1982.*

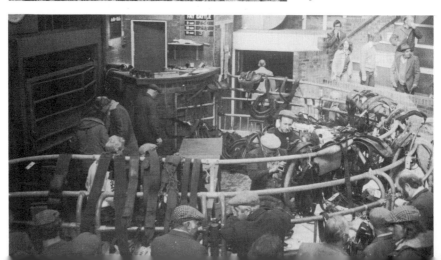

out the hazardous business of a wheeled vehicle trying to overtake the horse when going downhill. Village joiner Brian Alderson, of Gayle, Hawes, at the head of Yorkshire's Wensleydale, recently made his first farmer-ordered sledge for many years. Provided a reasonably long hitching chain is used, the sledge may be driven virtually anywhere that a horse can walk. The conveyance is easy and comparatively cheap to make, difficult to overturn, won't run away and is much less liable to slide sideways on a wet slope than is a rubber-tyred cart.

CITY HAULAGE

In circumstances very different from the moors of the south west and the Welsh hills, the heavy horse is again coming into its own. Interest for working horses on city streets has been so rekindled that in September 1981 the Shire Horse Society initiated an independent investigation into heavy horse haulage in the 1980s. The work was done by Ian Webster, BA (Econ), and London brewery teams helped launch its findings by adding colour to the official Press announcements at the Barbican.

Physical capabilities of heavy horses were summarised thus:

Payload A reasonable load for a heavy horse is twice its own weight. A pair working abreast can therefore haul four tons, and is obviously more economical than a single horse as only one driver is required rather than two.

Distance Ten to twelve miles a day is no hardship.

Hours of work Eight hours a day on heavy work is the maximum. Horses costed in the investigation were working only six hours a day, five days a week, 240 days a year. A six-day week causes no hardship.

Speed Where speed is vital, the heavy horse is unsuitable (emergency services, public transport). Nor is it useful where there is little payload and infrequent stops.

Terrain The use of a horse is limited in hilly areas, but these seldom occur in

Four horses and sixteen flashing white legs. Young & Co's team driven by Peter Tribe (Colin Fry).

towns. Vaux Brewery Percherons in Sunderland work some quite steep banks.

Weather Rarely effects town horses.

Summary Heavy horses are useful where the payload does not exceed four tons, where deliveries are within a five-mile radius and where speed is of secondary importance or is limited by other factors (eg, traffic). A high ratio of standing time to running time puts the horse to advantage.

Taking into account all factors — fodder, shoeing, depreciation, cost of replacement, wages, oil, sundries — the report makes a startling statement. 'There can be few commercial activities today where there is so little to choose, on a cost basis, between a system which is just about as intensive from start to finish as it was in 1881, and a system which is always striving to save labour. Heavy horse transport is competitive on a short haul basis and consideration should be given to the use of horses as a means of local transport', concludes the report.

Encouraging though this steady progress is, the heavy's real boom is on the show field. All sorts and conditions of men and women have bought a heavy horse for the sheer fun of feeding and grooming it, bringing it out as part of the summer show scene, comparing, making new friends and chatting after the event. Though the hobby is not cheap, it is a goal reached through giving up other things. A Suffolk may cost less than a new carpet and a Percheron less to maintain than a heavy smoker will spend. The one warning to be stressed is that these expenses will continue and that only the fortunate breeder may hope to break even. Prize money never equals expenses, even if you win the lot.

Chapter 2
On the land

Since they took over from oxen in the 18th and early 19th centuries, the horses' role on the land changed slowly and at times almost imperceptibly until the outbreak of World War 2. In the early years, their chief job was ploughing the land, harrowing it, and rolling in the sown seed. Then they carted the crops at haytime and harvest, and led roots home and farmyard manure out. But much seed was still sown by hand, and grass and corn were mown with a scythe.

The horses' work then altered with the introduction of corn and root drills, and the inter-row implements that quickly followed the latter. The biggest change of all came with the widespread use of the grass reaper and, later, the self-binder.

Today any radical innovation in farming techniques comes within the range of most farmers in two or three years. A century ago communications were poor, there was no agricultural Press as we know it, and of course no television or radio programmes. Money was even more of a limiting factor than it is now.

A magnificent farmyard study by J. F. Herring Jr from a 12 in by 18 in canvas owned by Arthur Ackermann & Son Ltd.

An ancestor of mine, brought up on a Pennines holding, said that when he was young in the 1860s to 1880s, summer was holiday time for the horses. He mowed grass with a scythe even in the early 1870s, though the reaper became standard equipment soon afterwards.

ANNUAL ROUTINE

The farming year begins in autumn. On a mixed arable farm, where a variety of crops was grown and a range of livestock kept, the first job for the teams after harvest was ploughing for wheat.

On reaching the field, the headland was marked out. To do this the plough was tilted and set so as to leave only a light furrow, little more than a scratch, all the way round the boundary and a precise distance, usually four or five yards, from it. The area so defined was known as the headland.

A ridge or rig was then set, choosing the longest and straightest side, and marking it with sticks or perhaps a white cloth hung in the hedge. Two shallow furrows were thrown out away from each other along the rig, then sandwiched together by means of deeper furrows, so that no unploughed ground remained between them. The team then ploughed round and round this mark in a right-

Jim Young's Percherons from Corringham, Standford-le-Hope, Essex, are well known in the show ring. Here they are ploughing at Correnham, Cambridgeshire and are driven by Dennis Hayter (Colin Fry).

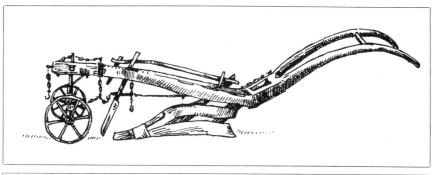

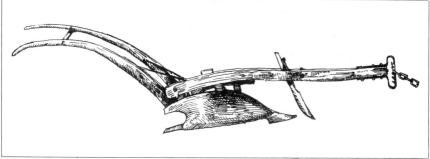

Top *Kent plough.*

Above *Wheeless plough, 18th century.*

Below *Warwickshire match plough.*

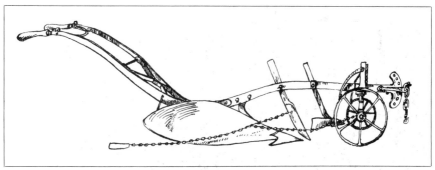

handed or clockwise direction until 11 yards had been covered, although the distance varied according to district and the type of soil.

Another rig was set parallel to the first, 22 yards away from it. It was ploughed round and round in similar fashion, the operation being known as 'gathering'. When that strip was 11 yards wide, the team turned left-handed each time the headland was reached, and worked anti-clockwise on the unploughed 11 yards-wide piece.

Known as 'harving out' or 'throwing out', that part of the operation continued with the team working steadily up and down until a narrow strip two furrows wide was left. This had to be parallel, and allowances made earlier to ensure a straight finish. The last two furrows were shallower than the rest, and perhaps only one horse would be used to 'take up' the last furrow, the other being tied to the hedge. A neat, straight finish was every ploughman's aim; if he failed, his work would be derided as 'like a dog's hind leg', or 'crippling every hare in creation'.

The wheat was sown by hand from a hopper or from a drill drawn by two horses. The furrows were harrowed down, a set of three harrows being enough for most two- or three-horse teams. If sown by hand the seed was flung on to the tight furrows, which made V-shaped drills, and then harrowed. If by a drill, the furrows were harrowed down first and harrowed in after the drill by a single pass with straight-toothed harrows.

Horse teams were used to lead the potato crop to clamps or pies made north and south along a headland, so that each side received some sun. Gangs of women

Right *Taking up the furrow, using one horse only, at the Northern Counties Ploughing Championships at Corbridge* (Gavin Cole).

Below *Nick Rayner's three Shire geldings and double furrow plough working in the rain. The driver is Eddie Dore* (Colin Fry).

*Shire mare and gelding disc harrowing on a farm at Wisley, Surrey. Owned by Mr Nick Rayner,
Hampshire.*

and children picked the crop into buckets or baskets, which they tipped into the
cart, the horse keeping pace by word of command. It was far pleasanter and
handier than working alongside a noisy tractor.

Sugar beet, mangels and turnips were similarly carted by the horse teams. In a
wet autumn it might be necessary to use a trace horse in front of the shafts, its
chains kept apart by a 'stretcher'.

When pulling the crop a worker stood between two rows, took a plant with his
left hand and chopped off the top with his right, dropping the topped roots to his
right. On reaching the headland, he turned right-handed and pulled another two
rows similarly dropping the roots on to those already topped. He then took the
next two rows, dropping the roots on his right, and turning round at the end so
that eight rows of mangels or turnips had been pulled and topped into two rows.
These two rows were just the right width to take a horse and cart, the horse
moving forward by voice command — no jumping on and off an awkward
tractor.

Heavy horses still have their place in difficult conditions. During the wet winter
of 1983, father and son Frank and Jim Elliot of Whamtown, Longtown,
Cumbria, had a heavy crop of swedes on ground so waterlogged that no wheeled
tractor could extract a load. Jim took his Clydesdale gelding Prince from the
championship ploughing team, yoked him to a cart, and hauled load after load to

Furrow press.

the cattle courts. Other farmers nearby had given up this bountiful crop due to tractors becoming bogged down in a wet season. Jim Taylor at Engine Farm, Morton Fen, Bourne, Lincolnshire, keeps a stud of Shires who on several recent occasions have saved the potato crop.

THE WINTER

As well as carting roots in, manure must be carted out. Frosty weather is ideal for this work. The standard for a single horse and cart was one ton, each horseman tipping or spreading his own load. A modern equivalent is the engine-driven manure spreader, hauled by a pair of horses.

Periodically during the winter, corn stacks would be threshed. This did not entail much horse work, except to cart the threshed grain to the railway station or mill, and to bring a load of coal for the steam engine. Either event called for a special show, bright horse brasses and newly-cleaned harness.

THE SPRING

If snow had held up land work for a period, the teams had to be 'fitted' before the spring rush. That is where the tractor scores; it can be switched off, left and started up weeks later with equal efficiency. The working horse, like an athlete, needs to be trained up to hard work again. So jobs like harrowing grassland were

sometimes undertaken, chiefly to give the horses something on which to test their muscles.

In spring the ploughing was completed, and as the land dried white under March winds, seedtime began. This was a very busy time for the teams; harrowing, pulling the heavy drill, leading out seed corn and fertilisers, dragging the rimmed Cambridge roller.

With the hedgerows bursting into new leaf and the birds singing, a spring morning on the land was very pleasant. The teams were eager for their work after a long winter of comparative inactivity, and the tearing sound of metal against soil and its newly-stirred smell were part and parcel of the horseman's day. The tractor driver can smell only fumes and even wears ear muffs to deaden sound.

Once the corn was sown the next drilling was sugar beet and mangels. Turnips followed later, well into May or June. The same two- or four-row drill was used for each, and root drilling was one of the most precise jobs in the farming calendar. If the rows were not straight and even, the horse hoes that followed would be liable to knock out some plants. The foreman often drilled the roots, always using the steadiest horse on the farm, for accuracy rather than speed was the aim.

Many an old mare has been kept in retirement and brought out simply 'to drill a few turnips'. She might well follow this up by 'side hoeing' the first time over. Metal discs fitted to the horse hoe or scruffler were set to shave the plants, and the closer the implement, the less tedious the hand hoeing.

Between drilling and side hoeing came a fairly slack time, for there was none of the spraying and dusting that now forms such a vital part of the farming scene. Once 'scruffling' started, however, it continued until the plants met in the rows in midsummer. A young horseman would take one of his pair in the morning, and the other in the afternoon, so they were always fresh. But no one ever thought of giving the lads a rest!

THE SUMMER

Root hoeing invariably continued into haytime, and the farmer had to decide which to do. Grass cutting with a pair of fast-stepping horses, nicely on top of their work, was more pleasure than work. This was especially so in the early morning when the rest of the world was asleep and the reaper whirred sweetly round and round the green meadow. Cutting at that time of day was far kinder on the horses than under noonday sun.

A variety of hay rakes, tedders and turners made the horse a busy animal doing work which had been done by hand in Victorian times. Sometimes the hay was 'swept' to a stack in the field, using a long-tined sweep with a horse at either side or singly. When full, the tines were tilted up and the load dragged to the stackside.

Top left *Robert Dash sowing fertiliser, drawing a Nicholson spreader at Spencers Wood, Berkshire (Colin Fry).*

Left *A spring-time cultivator drawn by a Clydesdale at Binfield, Berkshire. The driver is Alex Dedman of Hampshire (Colin Fry).*

Above *A print of the McCormick reaper of the early 1850s. It was the world's first practical harvesting machine.*

Top right *Hay making scene at St John's Chapel, Weardale, County Durham, c 1914* (Beamish Open Air Museum).

Right *Precursor of the self-binder. The old McCormick sail reaper at a modern Royal Show demonstration, drawn by two Suffolks* (Audrey Hart).

Bottom right *Cutting corn with a self binder. Three or four horses are usually needed for this job* (Gavin Cole).

There the handles were lifted, the points sunk in, and the whole apparatus tipped over.

THE HARVEST

The busiest time of all was harvest. A large team of horses was needed to haul a self-binder and it was indeed heavy work, particularly as the sun had to be high enough in the sky to dry the standing corn. Three and preferably four horses were needed. My grandfather used four, and changed two of them every hour, but on a small farm that was seldom possible.

No lover of the heavy horse can regret the tractor's arrival to haul the binder. In dry conditions and a nice, standing crop, the horses could walk away, but in a wet harvest, with the growing corn choked by a mass of green weeds, it was purgatory for the teams.

Leading home was another matter. The rustle of wheels across bright stubble, the smack of neat sheaves making up the load, the harvest scents, the walk home alongside one's favourite horse and the necessary breaks for 'drinkings' make a pleasant memory. When the tired Shires or Suffolks were turned out to pasture under a rising September moon, they bucked and rolled with new-found energy, snorting across pastures that might be mushroom-covered by morning.

Harvest and horses seem inextricably blended in so many childhood recollections. The sharp outline of the new stacks against the evening sky as we

A harvest scene from the Yorkshire Wolds early this century. Note the incredibly neatly thatched and trimmed row of round stacks. Each held half a day's threshing (Angela Mulliner).

returned from turning out the horses is another abiding memory. The skill that went into their making and thatching gave as much satisfaction as painting a fine picture and, if straw and sheaves rather than oils were the materials, the men who handled them undoubtedly qualified as artists.

In *The Old Country Squire* by P. H. Ditchfield is an account that highlights just how essential the heavy horse was to Victorian England. The year is 1850; squire John Whitmore Jones of Chastleton, Oxfordshire, had given up farming on his own account and was concentrating on the sporting side of his sizeable estate and the welfare of his tenants when a farm was thrown on to his hands by the sudden death of a tenant. Having no ploughs or cart horses of his own, he was in a quandary. He asked one or two neighbouring farmers as to how he could best cultivate his land and they immediately offered to give him a 'love hawl', if he would provide the seed corn and some bread and cheese and beer.

The day was fixed for the work to be done — April 6. The squire went up the hill to see the men at work, expecting to see a few plough teams. Imagine his surprise when he saw 68, and ten of them double teams! The horses were decked out in ribbons and the men wore clean white smock-frocks; altogether the scene looked like a gigantic ploughing match. One hundred acres were ploughed, harrowed and very nearly sown in one day; and great regret was expressed that the 'love hawl' had not been more widely known; if other farmers in the neighbourhood had heard of it, twice the number of teams would have been there.

Chapter 3
City work

Universal camera and film came too late to capture for us a long chapter of unparalleled horse history. The big cities, and London in particular, were served by an incredible number of horses in the final two decades of the last century. The omnibus companies alone had 10,000 horses around 1890. The Great Western Railway's Paddington Station was served by horses housed in a four-storey stable. The London coal trade needed 8,000.

Could we but step back 90 years, what an experience it would be for lovers of the heavy horse to visit those gigantic stables! The men who ran them were steeped in horse lore. W. J. Gordon in *The Horse World of London*, 1893, tells us about them.

> It is a novel experience being driven from yard to yard by one of the foremen in his gig. He had charge of about a thousand horses, and almost everyone he knew by sight, and could tell the stud it belonged to and place where it stood; and he was, apparently, posted in the history of every horse in every omnibus we met.
>
> 'See that nice little mare on the near side? A month ago she had paralysis in her back, but we pulled her through, we did. Here's a pair of big 'uns. The grey trod on a French nail, and a nice job we had to get the foot right. The near 'un had fever in the feet very bad last month; that isn't so serious; it is a very common complaint.'
>
> And with a lift of the whip elbow, answered by a similar lift on the part of the omnibus driver, we exchange the usual salute as we pass by.

VESTRY HORSES

There was one class of London horse unheard of today; even its name has been lost. The vestry horse was the refuse carrier, so called because such an essential service was first the responsibility of parishes. London produced 1,300,000 cart-loads of refuse a year, and required 1,500 horses to cope with the mass. They were big ones. Only really good cart-horses were up to the work, for one day they might have a 2-ton load, including the cart, on a good road, while on a wet day the draught might rise to 3 tons hauled over poor surfaces.

Most of these horses came from farms as mature and well-broken five-year-

Railway cartage horse.

olds. They weighed around 17 cwt, and almost every heavy horse county supplied them. Not every animal purchased as a vestry horse made the grade. It had to be able to back, and to back as readily as it went forward. Backing in the narrow streets of the time was as important as ability to side-step and avoid such hazards as glazed cellar lights. Average working life in vestry service was eight years, longer than omnibus or tram horses. Then, if lucky, the animal returned for a further spell of duty on England's green and pleasant land, finding relief in the furrows and the stubbles after so long on hard pavements.

On first meeting those unnatural roads with their constant bustle, the country-bred horse was usually sick for a week or so, until it became acclimatised. Then followed more training in backing, and shortly the new arrival was matched to its driver. A free-striding horse was put in the charge of a man of similar pace; a different animal would be chosen for a short man with choppy step, for they might spend years together and would be uncomfortable if not matched in step.

Though the vestry horse worked from 6 am to 5 pm, six days a week, it spent much of that time in accumulating a load rather than straining into the collar, so the life was not too arduous.

WATER CARTS

The horse hauling the water cart had the biggest starting pull of any horse in London. The conveyance weighed 1¾ tons and the water 2¼ tons. Though the 4

Barge horse.

tons total haul was usually short, it was often up a gradient, and the horses frequently suffered trouble with their forelegs.

COAL HORSES

Like the vestry horse, the coal horse came to London as a five-year-old. A big one was chosen, as a load of 3 tons including the vehicle was common. A four-wheeler was used for coal, so the horse did not have to take a strain on its back, but its journeys could be both long and uphill.

Breakfasting at 4 am, the coal horse began its round at six and did not return to stables until evening. A nose bag and a sack of bait provided the day's rations. Some of these coal horses were good enough to win acknowledgement in the Cart-Horse Parade, an event designed to encourage interest in good horse keeping among the thousands of employees. It has continued to the present as the Easter Monday Parade.

BREWERY HORSES

Of all London horses, the brewery teams were and are generally the best. They came as well-grown and well-made animals and filled out on an ample diet. 'Meat's a witch!', as dales farmers say, and brewery horse keepers had both the means and the ambition to put it into practice.

The brewers' dray of the 1890s carried 25 barrels of beer, each weighing 4 cwt

when full. That was 5 tons in total, and the dray itself weighed around 2 tons. The harness was not inconsiderable, and the men? One 29-year-old drayman of the last century scaled 20 st 10 lb, and not all today's are lightweights!

A total load of 8 tons may be fairly assumed, pulled by three horses. They were yoked unicorn fashion, two at the pole and one leader. The three had to be big and strong, approaching a ton each if not topping it, well-shod and in the prime of life. They were. Hoare's brewery, for example, did not possess a horse of under 17 hands or weighing less than 16 cwt. They were bought at six years old and disposed of at an average age of 12.

The placidity of these great horses was often remarked on. Regular work, feeding and care by the same men helped their natural dispositions, and their feet had individual attention. At Courage's there was no standard shoe; each horse had its own, and they were never thrown away, but mended by having an extra iron welded on again and again.

OMNIBUS HORSES

Omnibus, road car and tram horses all had short working lives, for hard roads and constant stopping and starting took early toll. The sunken tram rails became clogged with litter, adding considerably to the draught. The horses used could be classed as heavy vanners rather than pure-bred Shires or Clydesdales, for they provided the strength and weight which were needed for a two-horse car weighing over 5 tons when full of passengers. W. J. Gordon states that a gradient of 1 in 100 doubled the draught, and 1 in 50 trebled it.

To start a vehicle requires four or five times the power needed to keep it going,

Top left *At the London Easter Monday Parade* (Heavy Horse Magazine).

Left *London coal trolley.*

Bottom left *Modern Coalite dray followed by other trade turnouts in the Single Horse Turnouts at the Great Yorkshire Show, 1981* (Gavin Cole).

Below *The stable yard at Courage's Brewery* (Walton Adams).

These Suffolks pulling an old London omnibus are providing a lot of pleasure for a lot of people (Charles Goodsman).

and the road car averaged 500 separate stops and starts a day. Irregular stops and starts were made simply to suit the passengers; regular signed 'stops' were few.

London in 1890 had almost 10,000 tram horses, mostly working two-horse cars. These operated along 135 miles of tram line, of which 88 were double, and the 1,000 cars covered 21 million miles in a year. They carried 190 million passengers paying a million pounds in fares, the average fare per person being a penny farthing.

The basic unit was the 11-horse stud. All worked the same car in shifts. One horse worked round as relief, so that one was resting every day, and Sunday being a short day afforded the chance of a rest for three horses every seventh day. The car did five full trips daily, with a different team each time. The horses' working hours were therefore short, perhaps three or four hours, but they were arduous. The first cars left at 7.30 am, having been cleaned and checked during the night. One man cleaned seven cars on his shift.

Each stud was in charge of a horsekeeper, responsible for the forage and other bills. Maize, oats, beans and peas for 10,000 horses totalled 29,000 tons, in addition to bran and 20,000 loads of hay and straw. The average cost was 10s a week for a town horse's provender. An interesting method of tabulating feed costs at livery was so much per inch of height.

In the days when the horse was king, sales of horses were vital to the farm economy. As well as the working teams, harness horses were frequently bred. This is a Yorkshire Coach Horse.

CARRIAGE HORSES

The old North Riding of Yorkshire and adjacent parts of County Durham provided many London carriage horses. They were mainly Cleveland Bays or their offshoot, the Yorkshire Coach Horse. Though not strictly within the realm of heavy breeds, Cleveland Bays provided the main farm power on many farms in their area and were preferred by their advocates to the slower Shires and Clydesdales. Cleveland Bays of that era were claimed to be as strong as the heavy breeds, but they did not spread for farm work far beyond their birthplace. One farm worker told me that it was difficult to find a pair with even stride, one always tending to outpace the other; but I have heard no confirmation of the charge.

Clydesdales were also bred in the same areas and Clydesdale blood figured in the make-up of some of the carriage horses. A proportion were foreign, and to cater for the two-way Continental trade the Great Eastern Railway Company built stabling at Harwich for 80 horses.

COACHING

When coaching was at its height around 1835 there were 700 coaches at work, averaging ten miles an hour. This was far beyond the heavy horse's walking pace, but heavies often figured in the ancestry of coach horses, for the deplorable roads and the clumsy coaches required weight and strength from the teams.

The first mail coach appeared in August 1784 and Major Palmer, the Duke of Richmond's son-in-law, is credited with the idea of changing the horses every ten miles. Each horse ran for only one hour in 24, and had one day's rest in four. But the work was killing and four years in the job was the average any horse survived. Not until later in the 19th century did the more elegant, hunter-type of coaching horse become fashionable, its speed potential being realised through smoother roads.

THE JOBMASTER

A city dweller in need of a horse, whether regularly or infrequently, obviously lacked facilities. To meet this need the jobmaster sprang up and hired a huge selection of horses to a wide range of customers. He could also provide the conveyance, and an intricate scale of charges came into being. Some London jobmasters owned 50 pairs of carriage horses. In 1890-91 the administrative county of London issued 22,204 carriage licences. While the jobmaster provided many of the pleasure or status carriage horses, he kept in his ranks most types from a cob to a heavy dray horse. Nor was each family or firm confined to one town.

Tilling of Peckham had 2,500 horses in the early 1890s, from Cornwall to Brighton, and northwards to Sunderland. Peek Freans' biscuit vans were drawn by 100 Tilling horses.

The jobmaster was the safety valve. A private owner's single horse or pair might go sick or lame, and whether the master be milkman or doctor, his livelihood and

Men from all walks of life have taken their last earthly journey on a farm rulley. This scene shows the Duke of Devonshire's funeral.

the well-being of many people depended on his round. If the horse was 'jobbed', the risks were spread far wider, instead of being concentrated in the home stable.

THE FIRE BRIGADE

The heavy breeds frequently figure in the back-breeding of horses in jobs where strength and bursts of speed are needed, the fire-engine horse being an example. The late Victorian system of horsing fire-engines was a survival from the days when the brigade had the right to requisition any passing horses to drag the engine. Tilling had 60 fire-engine horses and 70 came from jobmasters in other parts of London. So the brigade often arrived with LCC written on its engine and TT on its blinkers!

COLOUR IN THE TOWN HORSE

'There can be no objection to good hard blacks' wrote Thomas Dykes, secretary of the Clydesdale Horse Society. He was speaking of colour in city horses of the 1890s and, had he lived 80 years later, would have been amazed at the fashion of black with four white legs that dominated the Shire world of the early 1970s. His choice was dark brown with black points, with bays of light or dark shades equally suitable. 'Greys when fully ripe, seem to be higher at the withers than others, while still retaining their gay carriage' was a keen Dykes observation, and he commented that red roans are generally noted for their great weight.

As an aside, one of the most useful and compact farm horses I have seen in recent years was a roan belonging to Mr Ted Dunning of Grange Farm, Whixley, York. The colour is now a Clydesdale one, but that mare would be an asset to any working stable.

'Blue roans are rarely handsome or captivating, but on the average they have more bone than the others, and are great favourites with some London horse owners on account of their hardy constitutions and tractable dispositions' wrote Dykes. 'For the hard wharfinger work off the Thames on the Middlesex side, where all is sheer hard horse toil in chains and shafts, they are greatly in use. In and about the mazy winds, and through the dark arches of Bermondsey you will come across them any hour of a hard working day, each and all walking at a faster pace than is allowed by the managers of brewery studs.'

The greys and blue roans of John Mowlem and Son, builders, were used for heavy stone hauling. The cement, timber and glazier and varnish trades preferred smooth-legged horses, upstanding like the Cleveland, or with the short, cobby Norfolk cart-horse characteristics. The latter trotted well under a medium load and lighter still were the beautiful, active horses of the pantechnicon vans, capable of trotting home with the empty van at seven miles an hour.

Lewis Berger and Son, starch manufacturers, preferred massive greys up to 17.2 hands, and 'not falling away below the knee as is sometimes seen in very heavy greys' as Dykes observed. Greys found a place in fire engines, the colour being conspicuous and apparently more fortunate than others in obtaining a clear road.

One type of working horse was always black, though it seldom comprised true heavies. Though coal horses were often black or dark bays, matching the coalman's clothes, the real 'black brigade' of London streets was made up of funeral horses. Job-masters specialised in the requisite type of horse just as others catered for pleasure outings or goods deliveries.

One stable on the East Road housed 80 Flemish horses, big, black and good-natured. A peculiarity here was that every horse was named after the celebrity, ancient or contemporary, most talked of at the time of his purchase, so General Booth, Huxley, Dickens and John Knox shared the same stable. An odd superstition arose from the use of church or chapel dignitaries' names. 'All the horses named after that kind of person go wrong somehow,' said the horsekeeper.

Mr Dotteridge, who headed a funeral firm, declared himself to be 'not a horsey man', yet he could assess a horse's nature by the peculiar glance it gave when looking round at him. He liked Roman noses, 'I never knew a horse with a Roman nose to be ill-natured'.

Another well-documented superstition was that the black horses became unhappy and restless if a coloured horse was stabled amongst them. If the same owner dealt in the different kinds, separate stables were used. The black funeral horses were tall, about 16 hands, and weighed 12 to 13 cwt. No great strength was needed, but an equable disposition combined with smartness was required.

Before British Rail cloaked stimulating rivalries under its universal umbrella, railway companies took special pride in selecting their own stamp and colour of horses. Glasgow draymen differed from London breweries in their horse types, favouring a muscular and more active, if not such a weighty, specimen. While the best London dray horses scaled 18 to 21 cwt, Glasgow's were 16 to 18 cwt. The latter were used singly, hauling $3\frac{1}{2}$ tons including the vehicle, while a London pair would move 5 tons and more. Liverpool had some of the best and heaviest, and the record pull with Shires was made there. There is a Liverpool bit and a Liverpool shoe.

Chapter 4
The Shire

'Studs situated in dry and light countries produce active, swift and vigorous horses, with nervous legs and strong hoofs; while those which are bred in damp places, have generally large heavy heads, thick legs, soft hoofs, and flat feet.' A late 18th century writer hands us the clue to our heavy breeds' derivation. Though there are undoubted references to the use of chariot horses by the Ancient Britons, these were probably of strong pony type and not heavies, but it was on such sound stock that the heavy stallions were used at a later date.

The Great Horse or war horse was the ancestor of our modern Shire and Clydesdale. From the Norman invasion of 1066 to the Battle of Bannockburn in 1314 it was a major instrument of conflict, that is a 250 year period — the equivalent of our looking back to the early 18th century. Suits of medieval armour prove that the war horse of those times carried up to 32 stones or 4 cwt, made up of the rider, his armour and the horse's protection. Only stallions were ridden and it is highly probable that they would be used, advertently or inadvertently, on likely mares in the neighbourhood.

Oxen provided much motive power on farms until the late 18th century, but even in 1145 we have records that 'Cart Horses fit for the dray, the plough, or the chariot were on sale at Smithfield, London, every Friday.' At Smithfield and other markets it was held that a horse 'with a cloud in his face', ie, with no star or blaze, was 'full of mischief and misfortune'. So false stars were made to put the matter right.

During King John's reign (1199-1216) 100 stallions 'of large stature' were brought across from the Low Countries, a link with this chapter's opening paragraph, for it seems that these giants were being developed on the plains of Western Europe, on land that was then often swampy. Such horses have been termed 'cold bloods', but it is an inapt description. Today's have enough mettle for anyone, and 'cold blood' or 'cart blood' is often used in derogatory fashion when describing one ancestor of a part-bred horse. It would be more accurate to ascribe the animal's bone, strength and docility as arising from the heavy breed influence.

Earlier cross-breeding occurred after the Battle of Bannockburn. Great Horses captured from the English knights were used on Scottish mares. The battle also affected future breeding policies in another way, because Robert the Bruce rode a 'palfrey' among the English heavies to such effect that the knights sought something faster and more manoeuvrable.

Information on the horse from this period until 1485, when Henry VII came to the throne, is sparse. Interest in horse breeding revived, and during that monarch's reign laws were passed prohibiting the export of mares worth more than 6s 8d, and of stallions. The object was to keep the best horses in the country. The practice of gelding is supposed to have begun about this time, which would have further effect in retaining only the best males for breeding.

The Great Horse of England reached another peak during the reign of Henry VIII. No stallion under 'fifteen handfuls' was allowed, but fortunately some remained in Wales and other wilder parts. Our love for the modern heavy does not blind us to the fact that there are 'horses for courses' and that a smaller pony with comparable appetite is much more suited to hill grazing.

In Elizabeth I's reign (1558-1603) the use of gunpowder spelled the end of the Great Horse in battle. It was still used to carry highly elaborate and heavy trappings on ceremonial occasions, an early instance of Sir Walter Gilbey's dictum that 'real worth in horseflesh is never put out of demand by the changes of man's habits; when it ceases to be of service in one respect it is sure to come into use in another.'

Charles I was another horse-loving monarch, but his predilection for racing and hunting led to a shortage of 'good and stout horses for its [the nation's] defence'. Cromwell's cavalry disdained even light armour and their success owed more to mobility than weight. The Great Horse was still favourite with the old regime, but its use turned towards coach, waggon and plough.

Even while yielding its place as a war horse, the Great Horse of England found a new niche. Stage coaches began to play an important part in transport. Their design was heavy and clumsy, the tracks which passed for roads were bad, and strong horses of great endurance were needed to pull them, especially in winter.

This short history suffices to stress that horse breeding has not been a story of slow but steady progress, but a series of see-saw movements with the heavy horse sometimes declining, sometimes ascending. We have recently passed through a dramatic decline, but are fortunate in taking part, whether as spectators or owners, in another great revival.

ROBERT BAKEWELL

By the late 18th century the Shire was approaching something like its modern form, though not its name. Robert Bakewell (1725-95) farmed Dishley Grange, Leicestershire, and bred cattle, sheep and horses. His raw material was the heavy black horse:

> In the fens of Lincolnshire, a larger breed of horses is produced than in any other part of this kingdom. Considerable improvements have, of late years, been made in this kind of horses by Mr Bakewell, of Dishley, and others; who, by great ingenuity and attention, have acquired such celebrity that they frequently sell stallions of their respective breeds for two hundred guineas.

The form of the black Lincolnshire horse has, by their management, been materially altered; the long fore-end, long back, and long thick, hairy legs, have been gradually contracted into a short, thick carcase, a short but upright fore-end, and shorter and cleaner legs.

The writer continues that horses of less bulk are required for farming systems then in vogue but that 'the black horse bred in the midland counties of England — ''a noble and useful animal'' — furnishes those admirable teams which we see in coal merchants', brewers', and other heavy carts and waggons about London, where the immense weight of the animal's body assists his accompanying strength to move the heaviest loads'.

That there were very heavy and very strong horses quite early in the 1800s is shown by the story of a wager near Croydon 'some years ago' (from c 1830) in which a common horse was to draw 36 tons for six miles along the Surrey Iron Railway, starting from a dead pull. That was over half a century before the first stud books appeared, so among the under-fed, badly stabled and sometimes ill-used animals there were horses of exceptional strength that provided the foundation for the breeds that developed in the late 19th century.

Bakewell was a friend of George Culley of Northumberland, a great chronicler of the period. Through the latter we glean much knowledge of Bakewell; not more than he deserves, but a disproportionate amount because of lack of records about his fellow breeders. Undoubtedly there was a very able knot of Midland breeders around that time. Among Bakewell's positive contributions was the importation of six Dutch or Flanders mares. This is interesting. Livestock breeders in early history, and some today, tended to seek improvement through the male side only.

There were at the time a Fen or Lincolnshire type of black, and a Leicester or Midlands type. Details are scarce; it is still not too late to hope that more may be unearthed. The Lincolnshire soil allowed full growth of bone and feather; Derbyshire limestone lent quality. Further west, Staffordshire heavies were mostly brown.

STUD BOOKS

We are now in the dawn of recorded Shire history, and the first positive stepping stone through this mire of speculation and mythology is the Packington Blind (or 'Blinded') Horse. He served mares in Derbyshire, Leicestershire and Warwickshire from about 1755 to 1770, and left some very good foals. If he hadn't, he wouldn't have been kept in his sightless condition.

Apparently he was black with white face and markings, stood on short legs and had good feet and pasterns. He was some 16.2 hands high (fully a hand lower than the average modern Shire stallion), was thick set and with a low forehand. Several of his many descendants combine in the pedigree of William the Conqueror 2343 in the Shire Horse Society Stud Book.

Before discussing the early retrospective volumes of the Shire Horse Society Stud Book, it is worth noting that the General Stud Book was compiled by Messrs Weatherby in 1791. This Bible of the Thoroughbred world was the first, to be followed by Coates' Herd Book for Shorthorn cattle in 1822. Another half century passed before the heavy horses, and most other livestock breeds, set down their genealogical records.

The English Cart Horse Society was formed in March 1878. Its early stud books contained retrospective entries relying on the memory of man, which was perhaps more reliable than some later records since proved incorrect! As samples of those retrospective entries we have K1191. (Stallions were given a stud book number, but mares were given name only until 1893.) K1191, foaled in 1820, was black with white hind legs and white on face, and owned by Joseph Lea, Burgh-in-the-Marsh, Lincolnshire. He was sired by Bakewell's horse B out of a dam sired by Bakewell's K. Agricultural writer and farmer William Marshall strengthens the link:

> The handsomest horse I have seen of this breed (the Leicestershire black cart-horse) and perhaps the most picturable horse of this kind bred on this island was a stallion of Mr Bakewell named K. He was in reality, the fancied War horse of the German painters; who in the luxuriance of imagination, never perhaps excelled the natural grandeur of this horse.
>
> A man of moderate size seemed to shrink behind his fore end, which rose so perfectly upright that his ears stood (as Mr Bakewell says every horse's ought to stand) perpendicularly over his fore feet. He died, I think, in 1785, at the age of 19 years.

Marshall continues: 'But the most useful horse I have seen of this breed is a much younger horse of Mr B whose letter I do not recollect. His carcass thick, his back short and straight and his legs short and clean; as strong as an ox; yet active as a pony.' Here is evidence that some very good horses had been bred in the late 18th century. 'Horse' in Bakewell's description above is synonymous with 'stallion', and was common usage at the time. The standard does not apply to the mare, whose graceful neck carries her ears further forward. But painters of the heavy horse today should bear in mind this portrayal from two centuries ago. Another interesting phrase is Marshall's 'as strong as an ox'. That has been handed down to us and is used unthinkingly today. When Marshall wrote it, he obviously had in his mind's eye the mighty cattle used in the plough teams of the time.

From 1795 to 1815 England and France were locked in bitter struggle. During this period land was ploughed which remained as grass or scrub during both World Wars. Yet cattle and sheep breeding proved so profitable that stockbreeders concentrated on them rather than on the horses. Then came a farming depression in which farmers sold what they could to survive, including their best horses. In any event hand rather than horse labour predominated and horse-drawn mowers had not then been invented.

Things picked up after 1837 and Queen Victoria's accession, with the English Agricultural Society being formed in 1838. Two years later it was granted its present name, the Royal Agricultural Society of England, and did sterling work in the 40 years before the Shire's own society was formed. Indeed since 1822 and the demise of the Board of Agriculture until the formation in 1889 of the

How the Shire used to look. Massive bone and feather were the breeder's aims.

Ministry of Agriculture, the RASE bore British farming's main organisational burden.

The early stud books furnish a wealth of information about the Shire's immediate ancestry and even about the times in which they lived. The brown Magnum Bonum was foaled in 1833, bred by Ullyatts at Parson Drove, Wisbech, Cambridgeshire, and had as grandsire True Briton and as great grandsire Honest Tom. Sherwood Ranger, a brown, was foaled in 1845 at Alfreton, Derbyshire, by Prince Albert out of a mare by Nelson Hero. That horse's sire Nelson 1617 first saw the light of day in 1824, one of 22 so named. It is reminiscent of 1981, when every other Clydesdale foal I met was called either Lady Di or Charlie! Incidentally, there were also 16 Napoleons in the first four Shire volumes.

It would be pleasant to look back on mid-Victorian days as serene and free from competition from the internal combustion engine. They were in fact an era of unenlightened feeding, scourged by hereditary diseases such as ringbones, sidebones, whistling, stringhalt, cataract and bone spavin. Farm workers had a hard time, enduring long hours, but the advent of steam power in mid-century did not diminish the need for work horses.

The 1850s were generally prosperous for British agriculture. Demand for heavy horses in towns was growing steadily; in 1865 the Great Northern Railway owned 820 horses, an appreciable number even though it trebled in the next 20 years. Unfortunately the lot of the many privately-owned town horses was lowered by damp, draughty stabling, lack of understanding and downright cruelty by drivers who themselves were hard put to survive. The contrast between the best and the worst run stables was equivalent to the then apparently unbridgable gap between wealth and poverty.

Wealth is often either an excuse for idleness or a springboard for great achievements. Fortunately for the Shire world, its rich patrons were men of the latter persuasion, and spared nothing in building up top-class studs. A mixture of rivalry, philanthropy and business sense was probably combined in their actions. Each, and his grooms, wanted his stud to be the best. Each had a then inborn duty to help tenants who, if they bred good, saleable Shires, were in a stronger position to farm and live well, and also to pay more rent to finance further improvements.

When the Earl of Ellesmere inherited his title aged 15, in 1862, he became owner of the 13,300-acre Worsley estate, near Manchester. Lying on top of great mineral wealth, the estate included a stud farm of 1,000 acres, and when the Earl came of age he appointed Captain Henry Heaton as manager of the Worsley Hall farms. The next year, 1869, the two visited the Royal Show at Manchester and bought the two-year-old colt Columbus. Within a twelvemonth the proven stock-getter Heart of Oak was acquired from Mr Thacker of Chatteris as an 11-year-old. Heart of Oak was Fen-bred, a weighty animal with $13\frac{1}{4}$ in of bone below the knee, a black that became one of the eight foundation sires of the modern Shire.

We cannot but envy the scope for rich men in those, for them, spacious days. The Earl of Ellesmere had over 100 horse boxes erected, open sheds with straw yards for the stallions, and grass paddocks for mares and foals. The stud was immediately successful in the show ring. By 1878 its numbers were outgrowing the capacious accommodation provided, and a draft sale, termed by his lordship 'weeding out', was arranged in February 1878.

THE SOCIETY IS FORMED

Readers may well be familiar with February 1878 as the date which marks the formation of the Shire Horse Society. It was no coincidence that after the sale the Earl talked to Frederick Street and asked him to propose the formation of a stud book association for their class of cart horse. Frederick Street was due to read a paper at the Farmers' Club, London, on the breeding and management of cart horses and the occasion was used to float the society. The Hon Edward Coke lent his full support and, spurred on by the knowledge that Suffolk and Clydesdale societies were being organised, the English Cart Horse Society was formed.

The Earl of Ellesmere's Columbus and a two-year-old colt Oliver had figured in an early co-operative horse breeding venture. The Bishop's Stortford Agricultural Horse Company was launched early in 1877 and its starting capital of £2,000 sufficed to buy the two stallions. With these two horses of known breeding, farmers on the Essex/Hertfordshire border could really set about improving their stock, especially as they had Messrs Walter Gilbey père et fils in their midst.

In 1822, breeders in the High Peak area of Derbyshire secured the services of

John Chadwick's five-year-old black Sovereign, a horse of Dishley antecedents. Fortunately Bakewell left many letters, from which it is clear that his stallions were frequently hired to groups of breeders rather than to individuals. But such loosely formed bands lacked the fibre to persist and to right wrongs, and fell by the wayside.

Others in those early days were the East Kent Cart-Horse Society and the South Devon Horse Association. Two Cornish bands of breeders had purchased two Clydesdale stallions at £300 apiece. It should be stressed that these events took place before the stallion hiring system had been thought out. There was no insurance, so if the horse did not do his job well through any cause, the group suffered a dead loss.

THE SCOTTISH HIRING SYSTEM

In the late 1860s the Glasgow Agricultural Society organised a central stallion hiring fair, replacing the old method whereby stallions were walked from one local event to another in the hope of enticing customers among the different hiring societies. These had been part of the Scottish scene since the 1830s.

Such small societies used a variety of methods. Some hired the stallion at a set fee for the season, collecting individual stud fees themselves. Others charged the mare's owner a fee when she was served and a further fee when she was shown in-foal, guaranteeing a minimum number of mares, usually 80. A third method was to offer a premium and reduced service and foaling fees, but not guaranteeing a minimum number of mares. One great advantage of the system was that if the stallion became incapacitated from any cause, any reputable owner could and would replace him. For the hirers, this was a big step forward compared with an outright purchase and no redress.

THE MONTGOMERYSHIRE SYSTEM

The first tentative steps towards organised hiring and fairly strict rules came from Wales. The Montgomeryshire District Heavy Horse Society selected its first stallion in 1876 through holding a show with a prize of £100. In the following year a deputation travelled around a number of studs, and selected England's Wonder from Charles Marsters in Norfolk. This horse was one of the best in England, nicknamed 'Old Strawberry' by farmers grateful for the roan foals he left. Thus even before the Shire Horse Society was formed, Montgomeryshire breeders were establishing an enduring superiority.

They were followed by Crewe, and later by others, till a network of stallion hiring societies covered the country. Many fell by the wayside after World War 2, but others have regenerated. For combining business with pleasure it is hard to beat a day out with a band of heavy horse breeders seeking next year's stallion and being regaled with ample food and drink as they go!

CHAMPIONS

There is near the Lancashire coast a district of black soil not dissimilar to the Fens, where today horticulture predominates. The Fylde has another claim to fame in the quality of Shires bred there, which started in the early 1870s with those twin pillars of Victorian rural England, the squire and the parson.

Parson Wood became mentor of the young squire Thomas Horrocks Miller, and together with a few local landowners they organised the Fylde Cart-Horse Breeding Improvement Company in 1869. The object was to help tenant farmers to supply home-bred cart horses for the apparently endless needs of the Lancashire industrial towns. The infant Improvement Company started with a stallion called Carbinier. Although a good horse, he was not the best in England, and there the ambitious young squire's aims lay.

A stallion that had proved himself not only in the show ring but through the soundness of his stock was Honest Tom 1105. The number is important; there are 69 Honest Toms in Volumes I-IV of the Stud Book! William Welcher had bred this Honest Tom at Snare Hill, Watton, Norfolk in 1865, the farm name being indicative of the rabbit-ridden state of stretches of East Anglia when the farm was laid out. The horse had taken first prize at the Royal Show for five years in succession, 1867-71, and squire Miller had to pay 500 guineas before his breeder could be tempted to part with him.

Honest Tom moved to Singleton and the Fylde, and in 1872 repeated his Royal Show successes for his new owners, thereby bringing his total winnings to £526 15s, including £145 for the six Royal Show firsts. A 1983 Royal Show Shire winner in a class of six to ten horses received only £30.

Some of Honest Tom's colts were retained for breeding, but even those for draught made far more than the £12 to £15 that had previously been the rule. Honest Tom gave a boost to horse-breeding farmers' incomes and built a firm foundation for Fylde Shires that has been retained ever since. Their successes spurred these Fylde Shire men to support the new stud book movement, thereby influencing progress of the whole breed.

A Lancashire horse, Admiral 71, won the London championship in 1880 for the Earl of Ellesmere. James Forshaw of Blyth, Nottingham, won with Bar None two years later, establishing a top place which his family held for many years. Two sons of William the Conqueror won in 1885 and 1886. They were Prince William and Walter Gilbey's Staunton Hero and then in 1887 came Harold's triumph. Tom Forshaw described Harold as 'a beautiful dark brown, with broad white face and white hind legs to the hocks. Standing 17.2 hands, he was a majestic horse in carriage and movement, and would weigh about 21 cwt.'

In 1888 the top London horse was Prince William, but he stood above Harold and Hitchin Conqueror only because no judge could admit to not being able to part the first three. Within 50 years every registered Shire in the country, and many unregistered ones, would go back in male tail to one of these three stallions. Incidentally, 61 stallions lined up for the three-year-old class, won by Harold's earliest prize winning son All Here.

There followed a string of classic names. Yet another Lancastrian horse, Vulcan, took the 1889 title. Descendants of his breeder John Whitehead of Medlar Hall, Kirkham, are still enthusiastic Shire people today. The Earl of

Ellesmere showed Vulcan, who won again two years later.

Sandwiched between those successes was Hitchin Conqueror, another William the Conqueror son, in 1890. Then in 1892 Bury Victor Chief gained the title for Joseph Wainwright of Chapel-en-le-Frith, Derbyshire. The horse had won the Royal Show championship the year before, and was bought by Mr Wainwright from John Rowell for an astonishing 2,500 guineas. Bury Victor Chief regained the London title in 1894, splitting the wins by Rokeby Harold in 1893 and 1895-96.

The Harold line continued to dominate until the new century was born through Markeaton Royal Harold and Buscot Harold, the latter gaining his third successive triumph in 1900.

The new century got into its stride with Stroxton Tom, Birdsall Menestral, Girton Charmer (sounds like a mare's name) and Tatton Dray King. Gaer Conqueror and Champion's Goal-keeper each had successive victories until the guns that overturned the ordered world began to rumble.

This list of champion stallions at the London Show from 1885 to the outbreak of war in 1914 reads like a list of giants, each with his niche in an era of Shire greatness.

FEATHERY LEGS

The old century was in its last year when a foal was born that was to change Shire horse fashions for half a century, and whose attributes are still harked back to in the 1980s.

Lockinge Forest King was of impeccable lineage. He also had substance and character but, above all, hair. The hair or feather on his fore legs sprouted at the black knees, and from only just below the hock on his snowy white hind legs. Not

One of the old sort. An unknown, heavy-boned Shire stallion imported into the USA around the turn of the century.

The Duke of Devonshire obviously favoured best Shire stallions for his tenants.

only was he thus endowed, but he passed on the same hairy attributes, which was why he had many descendants. In the early 1900s a heavily feathered Shire sold for more than a fine-haired one, and today's comparatively silky haired horses would have been laughed to scorn by Edwardian horsemen.

'The British stockbreeder can breed anything in the world if there's money in it.' When the demand was there, Swaledale sheep breeders transformed their flocks from grey faces to jet black and the legs from white to mottled, in a few generations. Pig breeders produced incredibly long, lean baconers, cattle breeders a tight udder that withstood machine milking. And all because it paid.

A Shire with hairy legs certainly paid in those pre-1914 days when grooms were plentiful and cheap, hard work a virtue and hair was equated with bone. Lockinge Forest King provided hair in such profusion that the highly skilled grooms of the period could enhance a good leg with it, and disguise a poor one.

Chivers pointed out that the horses would look very different if they were walked through a pond before sale, but they were not. They were paraded, all brushed out and dry, and doctored with resin and other noxious substances that gave the impression of masculinity, but affected the genes not at all.

The reason that Lockinge Forest King was so prepotent for hair becomes apparent in studying photographs of his ancestors. His great-grandsire was Lincolnshire Lad, whose son the grey Lincolnshire Lad II had masses of hair high up his legs. The bay Lockinge Forest King was bred by Lady Wantage at Lockinge, and later owned by J. P. Cross, Catthorpe Towers, Rugby and then by W. T.

Hosing down a Shire's feet before sale, watched by a horseman of the old school.

Everard, of Bardon Hall, Leicester. He won a string of notable prizes, and begat offspring that won cups and rosettes by the score. More important, the male descendants of this great stallion sired foals that sold at well above the average then obtaining, making it a business proposition for farmers to pay a handsome stud fee for their services, and therefore for the stallion owners to vie with each other in obtaining Lockinge Forest King sons and grandsons.

THE GREAT WAR AND AFTER

The world conflict of 1914-18 ended the era of unlimited skilled labour. Grooms and their horses died together in Flanders, where massive animals were less well adapted to the horrific conditions than cleaner-legged ones.

A flood of 'demobbed' horses poured on to the market at the War's end, as uncontrolled as the mass of soldiers seeking in vain for 'the land fit for heroes', or even a job of any sort. The number of entries in the Shire Horse Society stud book reached its all-time peak in 1920 and 1921, but not until the late 1920s did the position sort itself out, and demand and supply of draught horses reach some sort of equilibrium.

In the poverty-stricken countryside that existed until the mid-1930s, the best Shire studs kept their heads above water, but usually from outside finance rather than horse breeding. The big shows still attracted large classes, but there was no spare cash for experiment and survival rather than improvement was the order of the day.

A feature of the Shire scene from the outbreak of World War 2 until the slaughter of the late 1940s was the succession of notable grey stallions. They made up over one third, 77 out of 211, registrations in the 1944 Stud Book, which incidentally included four roans. In 1948 the two-year-olds at the Derby Shire Horse Society Show included three greys among the six two-year-old stallion prize winners, two among nine three-year-old top stallions, three of the best seven four-year-olds, and four out of nine winning senior stallions.

Of the eight pairs of heavy horses of Shire type at the 1948 Spring Show, three pairs were greys, including the dapple greys Manea Duke and Manea Prince from G. C. Bedford. A portent was to be found in the fours, both entries being all blacks. Young & Co's Brewery Ltd and Francis L. Bowley were the stalwarts giving the crowds a revival of memories after five years of war and shortages.

The decade following peace in 1945 is a rather neglected period in Shire history. Though the breed was in numerical decline, there was still much activity among the top studs and some excellent horses in evidence. Notable among these was The Bomber, who won the 1949 Derby Show (then the chief Shire event) for Dick Sutton.

The Bomber combined the best of the old and modern types. A brown with three white legs and the off-fore black, he stood 17.2 hands high, and presented himself perfectly. He was bought in Crewe by R. G. Thompson as a three-year-old, for 650 guineas, having been bred by J. Kirkland at Belper, Derbyshire. He was used in Lancashire for two seasons, was bought by Dick Sutton and let to the Uttoxeter Society before serving mares on Anglesey. At the time there were three heavy horse societies on the island.

At that 1949 show The Bomber was eight years old. 'One of the greatest Shire stallions ever' is Herbert Sutton's recollection. He 'travelled' the stallion, not by walking, but by using a motor wagon, returning to stables each evening and setting off with a fresh horse next morning. Even in 1951-52, Suttons' stallions were covering 200 mares a season. Most stallion hiring societies continued to operate until about 1955.

One of the most important post-World War 2 sales took place when Freshneys dispersed their stud. Dick Sutton bought the stallions Bengie and Great Hope for 685 and 640 guineas, quite a lot of money then. Our William went to Balderstones and Cumbers (later to found the Royal Show John Cumber Park) acquired Our Surprise for over 600 guineas.

All these horses were by Raans Record Ways, son of Raans Record. They included Woburn Dustman, who went to Suttons for 120 guineas and did as well as his more expensive brethren. As an old horse, Dustman was travelled in Lancashire by R. G. Thompson of Blackpool. He was foaled in 1938 at Woburn Abbey where the Duke of Bedford's stud was stabled. Dustman had three white legs and a white patch on his body, so not all white patches on Shires can be blamed on Clydesdale imports of the 1960s! Raans Record, incidentally, takes us another big jump back to 1929, where this brown horse with the broad stripe down his face, and four white legs, was bred by William Clark at Raans Farm, Amersham, Buckinghamshire, winning prizes as a foal.

Bengie's 680 guineas' cost was recouped when he was hired to the Uttoxeter Shire Horse Society for three seasons at 600 guineas a season. This was followed by two years with the Welshpool and one with the Fylde Societies. Great Hope went to Crewe, at over 500 guineas the season.

A horse that left a lot of winners in the early 1950s was Polwarth Spellbinder. He headed the two-year-old stallions at Peterborough in 1960. Herbert Sutton, who travelled him, said: 'Spellbinder would have done well today. He was a 'modern' horse, with clean limbs and fine hair. He was hired from Bob Fish of Scotton, Lincolnshire, and I handled him for my uncle, Dick Sutton.'

A black that John Richardson tried unsuccessfully to buy was Preston King Cole. He was by Edingale What's Wanted and was hired to Welshpool in 1953. He also served mares for the Brigg, Lincolnshire, Society.

Terms for Dick Sutton's Preston Shire Stud stallions in 1953 were £4 10s for each mare. Clients requiring a stallion other than on his normal route were charged 10s extra and mares barren from the 1952 season (to Sutton's horses) had their fees reduced to £2 10s. The groom's fee was 5s, to be paid at time of service, though for many years the groom's fee had been half a crown.

In 1953 the Preston stud listed 26 stallions, in addition to those hired to societies, so heavy breed stallions were still big business. There is a sad little obituary to The Bomber; 'Top Stud Horse in England when he died'.

Althorpe Trump Card triumphed at Derby in 1947 and 1948. He was shown by those Shire stalwarts J. & W. Whewell, probably best remembered through Heaton Majestic, eight times champion gelding in the dark days of the 1960s. The grey Crimwell Quality was female champion in the three years 1948-50.

There is a strong temptation to skip heavy horse history in the late 1950s and throughout the 1960s. Homage is due to those stalwarts who carried the tattered flag, however, and there are horses of note whose blood has figured strongly in the resurrection. The last hardbacked Shire Horse Society stud book was the combined volume 1957-59. Then came the loose leaf era; no photographs, no lists of winners, no officials' or judges' names, in fact just the bare registrations.

They were bare indeed; the five volumes 82 to 86, clipped narrowly together, contain less than a hundred stallion names. Winners return in 1963, augmented by photographs in 1964, when S. G. Garrett's Carr Coming King was champion and a yearling stallion named Ladbrook What's Wanted foretold his future for Arthur Lewis. In 1965 Carr Coming King stood second among the five senior stallions to the champion, John Suckley's Alneland Delegate, a brown showing indications of Clydesdale breeding. But no matter; he was a grand stud horse. In that year the 17 in-hand geldings numbered one more than the combined numbers of yearling and two-year-old fillies. Today the number of geldings has fallen disproportionately low.

By 1966 names familiar in modern pedigrees appeared; Grange Wood Clifford and Grange Wood William, Edingale Draughtsman, with Grange Wood Bengie as reserve to the champion stallion, Ladbrook What's Wanted. In 1967 only 28 stallions were registered but they included the grey Alneland Masterpiece, the bay Bellasize Select, Hainton Warrant, and Jim's Chieftain who set the seal on

Left *Happy scene at the end of the Bisquit Cognac Shire Horse of the Year Award, Wembley.*

Bottom left *The roan Shire gelding Broadley Monarch foaled in 1972 who won 44 cups in one year (Gavin Cole).*

Right *Harnessing a Shire gelding at Samuel Smith's Brewery, Tadcaster, Yorkshire.*

American revival when bought by Arlin Wareing, Blackfoot, Idaho. Young's showed an eight and Courage, Barclay and Simonds a six.

Even in 1970 only 33 Shire stallions were registered. Not till 1973 do they indicate a firmer footing, with 77 registered. By 1981 88 colt foals were notified in addition to the 50 stallions registered.

CHAMPIONS TODAY

The senior stallions at the 1983 Peterborough Shire Horse Show were names to conjure with. So were the progeny group sires, stallions competing for the Walter Gilbey Memorial Prize for the best group of three animals of either sex, but not gelded, by the same living sire. They were headed by Arthur Lewis' black Ladbrook Aristocrat, a former Supreme Championship stallion, and by that wonderfully free-moving bay, L. Jones' Quixhill Masterpiece, then 11 years old. Among others on the list of honour through their offspring was the black Bulbridge Traveller, his showing career curtailed by an accident, but who was a great favourite of Arthur Lewis before being bought by C. J. Webb, Wiltshire.

The show champion stallion, Cubley Charlie, owned by J. & E. Salt, was listed in catalogue order next to Edingale Mascot, by Grangewood William and almost as legendary as his owner, 'Jos' Holland of Tamworth, Staffordshire, whose award of the MBE in the 1983 New Years Honours won acclaim throughout the heavy horse world.

Greenhaulme Premier King, of Stanley House blood, will be remembered for his daughter Greenhaulme Chosen Girl, a 1982-83 Shire Horse of the Year highlight. Then came Hainton Jim, from E. Cosgrove & Son in Lincolnshire. We passed the Hainton establishment one May evening, and saw a field with into the 'teens of Shire mares and foals. Seldom have I so regretted having an appointment elsewhere!

Hainton Jim's two sons were catalogued next. Metheringham Duke has already sired a colt full of promise, Gorefield George, while Metheringham Joseph showed quality breeding through his dam Tremoelgoch Beauty and her sire the great Grangewood Benjie. Raygold Bill sported Hainton blood, while Ryefield Select was sold at John Suckley's Alneland dispersal sale.

Closing the alphabetical list was Skelton Masterpiece, by Alneland Masterpiece, and with grandsire Crossfield Supreme on his dam's side. Many of the top names among Shires of the 1960s and '70s are included in this wonderful class and the stallions' pedigrees.

CHARACTERISTICS OF THE SHIRE

SIZE

'The largest horse in Britain' is a title that has been awarded to the Shire. It is doubtful if any one breed can now claim that distinction. Individual animals of all four main British heavy breeds at the optimum age and condition can turn the scales at well over a ton, and a very big horse is needed to do that. Percheron stallions have reached massive weights; Clydesdale entries that circle the Scotstoun ring have giants among them, and the Suffolk produces taller animals than a few years ago. We must content ourselves by saying that the Shire contains some of the biggest in the heavy horse world.

Though weight is needed to move weight, mere height is not necessarily a desirable characteristic in pulling a load. The taller the animal, the higher the point of draught, and top-class engineering brains including Brunel have not been slow to point out that the lower the point of draught, the more efficient the pull. Nevertheless, as a spectacle the big 'uns are difficult to beat, and in America tall, flashy Belgian geldings of 19 hands high are very valuable indeed. That trait may follow so many others across the Atlantic. Don't forget when picturing these goliaths that any man below medium height has difficulty in stretching up to touch the top of the shoulder or withers (the measuring point) of a 19 hands horse.

Though a Shire stallion's minimum requirements are a height of 16.2 hands, very few today are under 17 hands, and the average is put at 17.2 hands. A fair proportion of mature stallions top 18 hands.

COLOUR

This is defined simply as black, brown, bay or grey. Neither roan nor chestnut is allowed in the stallion. There is every justification for barring roan, which is a Clydesdale colour, but many Shire enthusiasts would like to see chestnut animals. The breed has an early record of chestnut champions. Chestnuts won three of the five stallion classes at the first breed show at Islington in 1880. Czarina won the supreme female championship in 1884. She was a chestnut three-year-old, described as 'a wonder for her age; immense substance, depth of rib, length of quarter, flat bone, fine quality of hair, good feet, and for so heavy a filly, fine action which renders her an animal in every way fitted to receive honours as a champion female of the Shire breed'.

An interesting aside is that Czarina's owner, the Hon Edward Coke, Society President in 1881, named all his Shires with the initial letter C. Czarina's sire was a bay, Helmdon's Emperor. All we know of her dam is that she was by England's Glory 745, who was a bay by England's Glory 733 (also bay, foaled 1860) out of a mare by Golden Ball 948, who was a brown.

For the first 20 years of Shire Horse Society history there was no prejudice against chestnuts. After 1900 they declined in popularity, but a chestnut was still right to the fore in 1912 and again in 1913, when Dunsmore Chessie claimed the supreme female championship, as a four-year-old and a five-year-old.

In the early 1970s black with four white legs was the fashionable colour. Undeniably flashy, it has the further advantage that black is easy to match. Though the intensity of black may vary, it does not show the same range as bay, from very light to very dark. A bay by definition has black mane and tail. If the mane and tail are brown, it is classed as a brown. In the 1982 Shire Horse Society Show there were 30 browns out of a total entry of 294.

Grey is another colour showing a wide range of shade, with the added complication that greys tend to go lighter with age. The range of greys normally accepted by horsemen is dappled, steel, iron, black and flea-bitten. An advantage of grey is that there is no difficulty matching face or leg markings. (A black or brown may have anything between no and four white feet.) Greys also look very smart in contrast against a green-painted vehicle.

A white Shire is very rare, but has been registered.

FEET AND HAIR

The hair covering the feet, known as 'feather', is now defined in the standard as: 'Not too much; fine, straight and silky'. This contrasts dramatically with Shires around the turn of the century, when hair was the god before which all other characteristics bowed. There was and is sharp divergence of opinion among breeders whether bone, which all desire, can be bred without heavy feathering.

Without doubt the Shire has been greatly 'cleaned up' in the leg since World War 2 by introduction of Clydesdale blood. This is a contentious issue, but most breeders find that the cleaner leg is better suited to modern conditions. Skilled grooms are no longer cheap, plentiful and prepared to work all hours. In fact the owner is usually the groom today.

STANDARDS

The standard for the modern Shire is as follows:

Stallions

Colour Black, brown, bay or grey. No good stallion should be splashed with large white patches over the body. He must not be roan or chestnut. *Height* Standard 17 hands and upwards. Average about 17.2 hands. *Head* Long and lean, neither too large nor too small, with long neck in proportion to the body. Large jaw bone should be avoided. *Eyes* Large, well set and docile in expression. Wall eye unacceptable. *Nose* Slightly Roman, nostrils thin and wide; lips together. *Ears* Long, lean, sharp and sensitive. *Throat* Clean cut and lean. *Shoulder* Deep and oblique, wide enough to support the collar. *Neck* Long, slightly arched, well set on to give the horse a commanding appearance. *Girth* The girth varies from 6 ft to 8 ft in stallions from 16.2 to 18 hands. *Back* Short, strong and muscular. Should not be dipped or roached. *Loins* Standing well up, denotes good constitution (must not be flat). *Fore-end* Wide across the chest, with legs well under the body and well enveloped in muscle, or action is impeded. *Hind-quarter* Long and sweeping, wide and full of muscle, well let down towards the thighs. *Ribs* Round, deep and well sprung, not flat. *Forelegs* Should be straight as possible down to pastern. *Hindlegs* Hocks should not be too far back and in line with the hind-quarters with ample width broadside and narrow front. 'Puffy' and 'sickle' hocks should be avoided. The leg sinews should be clean cut and hard like fine cords to touch, and clear of short cannon bone. *Bone measurement* Of flat bone 11 in is ample, although occasionally $12\frac{1}{2}$ in is recorded — flat bone is heavier and stronger than spongy bone. Hocks must be broad, deep and flat, and set at the correct angle for leverage. *Feet* Deep, solid and wide, with thick open walls. Coronets should be hard and sinewy with substance. *Hair* Not too much, fine, straight and silky.

A good Shire stallion should stand from 17 hands upwards, and weigh from 18 cwt to 22 cwt when matured, without being overdone in condition. He should possess a masculine head and a good crest with sloping, not upright, shoulders running well into the back, which should be short and well coupled with the loins. The tail should be well set up, and not what is known as 'gooserumped'. Both head and tail should be carried erect. The ribs should be well sprung not flat sides, with good middle, which generally denotes good constitution. A stallion should have good feet and joints, the feet should be wide and big around the top of the coronets with sufficient length in the pasterns. When in motion, he should go with force using both knees and hocks, which latter should be kept close together; he should be straight and true before and behind. A good Shire stallion should have strong character.

Mares
Colour Black, brown, bay, grey, roan. *Height* 16 hands and upwards. *Head* Long and lean, neither too large nor too small, long neck in proportion to the body, but of feminine appearance. *Neck* Long and slightly arched, and not of masculine appearance. *Girth* 5 ft to 7 ft (matured) according to size and age of animal. *Back* Strong and in some instances longer than a male. *Legs* Short, with short cannons. *Bone measurement* 9 to 11 in of flat bone, with clean cut sinews.

A mare should be on the quality side, long and deep with free action, of a feminine and matronly appearance, standing from 16 hands and upwards on short legs; she should have plenty of room to carry her foal.

Geldings
Colour As for mares. *Height* 16.2 hands and upwards. *Girth* From 6 ft to 7 ft 6 in.

Bone measurement 10 to 11 in under knee, slightly more under hock and broadside on, of flat hard quality.

A gelding should be upstanding, thick, well-balanced, very active and a gay mover; he should be full of courage, and should look like, and be able to do a full day's work. Geldings weigh from 17 to 22 cwt.

Chapter 5
The Clydesdale

Where ploughland meets the heather
And earth from sky divides
Through the misty northern weather
Stepping two and two together
All fire and feather
Come the Clydes!

That was Will H. Ogilvie's idea of Scotland's national heavy horse. It strides out with a smart clip-clop in which each hoof swings beyond the perpendicular, so that when viewed from behind the full face of the metal shoe is seen, and hind leg action is such as to remind the onlooker of a Scotsman wearing a kilt with a bit of a swagger!

The Clydesdale reached its zenith, as did our other heavy breeds, in the early 1920s. In fact, the stud books for the years 1919, 1920 and 1921 have a combined width of almost seven inches, and contain the new registrations of 5,000 mares and 700 stallions.

The preceding chapter described how heavy stallions from the Low Countries were used on native pony mares to throw a bigger and stronger foal. Precisely the same happened north of the Border, only the pony breeds being different. They were chiefly Highland and the 'Galloway nag' which Shakespeare in *King Henry IV* termed 'a certain race of little horses in Scotland ... lighter for hunting'. The imported stallions stamped changes on a very sound native horse, short in the leg, active, stout and clean in the limb. That is the centuries-old foundation.

From mediaeval times onwards there was an influx of heavy horses into Scotland directly from the Low Countries, and indirectly via England. The Duke of Hamilton in the late 17th century is credited with introducing six stallions from Flanders, although Aiton of Strathaven claims that people living in the district at the time had no recollection of them, which seems quite inconceivable if they really were there. Then John Paterson of Lochlyoch introduced a black Flemish stallion from England and started a heavy horse stud somewhere around 1715 to 1720. We may reasonably assume that he was not the only one, merely the best documented.

No one concerned with breed histories should omit the effect of changes in the rest of the agricultural scene. Horse breeders did not plan their matings for the benefit of future historians; they considered them according to the needs of the times. The needs of arable farmers as the 18th century wore on were for more powerful, swift-stepping horses to provide motive power for new implements. Small's iron swing plough (or wheelless plough) was introduced in 1763. It was driven, as have been single furrow ploughs ever since, by one man and pulled by two horses. Before that, eight to twelve oxen and four men had been required for the very heavy old wooden plough.

By 1791 all the 40 teams entered in a ploughing match at Alloa were using ploughs of Small's design. That is almost 30 years after its invention. A similar breakthrough today would be considered by 90 per cent of farmers in the country within two years. Means of communication then were pioneered by the Highland and Agricultural Society of Scotland, who granted Silver Medal awards to encourage better ploughing. Ploughing matches became the order of the day and as the art of ploughing spread, so did the blood of the best horses.

In early Victorian times farming was prospering and travelling stallions were sent from the Clyde valley, the cradle of the breed, to all parts of Scotland. Symon tells us of that time: 'The sight of a well-matched, well-groomed, spirited pair of

Arthur the Clydesdale in Kielder Forest. The 'stretcher' keeping the trace chains apart is clearly shown as is the method of harnessing and yoking (Gaving Cole).

Clydesdale stallion.

Clydesdales in shining harness was most pleasing to the eye'. According to Trow-Smith, heavy horse breeding became one of the main occupations of farmers in the counties immediately north of the Border. Breaking in was done by other farmers from Renfrew and Ayr, who bought foals from the breeders at Lanark and Carnwath fairs, trained them to five-year-olds and then resold them at Rutherglen and Glasgow fairs to eastern Scotland and northern England.

We are now moving towards the period when the Clydesdale Stud Book was envisaged, on the model of that classic of the Shorthorn world, Coates Herd Book. The Clydesdale Horse Society was formed in 1877 and in its first or retrospective volume, 1878, we trace back through 'the memory of man' to the first half of the 19th century. For example, Lofty (453), was a light brown, foaled about 1825 and bred at Longtown just south of the Border, and never beaten but by his son Young Clyde. His sire was Old Stitcher (574), foaled about 1818, and described as a bright bay. The one great female chieftain of the Clydesdale race was, according to leading breeder Dunlop, Knox's Rosie, foaled in 1869. 'The heaviest, big, compact, good-looking draught matron that ever graced any exhibition. And of course she had a good dash of Shire blood in her.'

The Shire admixture is readily acknowledged by several top Clydesdale men early this century. William Dunlop, writing in 1935, stressed: 'Our Clydesdales so named and Shires are not really two breeds at all, but practically one breed. The kings and queens of the Clydesdale to begin with were nearly all first cousins with the Shire. There is no section that can claim to be a pure breed in the strict interpretation of the term. The draught horse of the British Isles is a type and not a breed (it is a good thing there were no Suffolk men in his audience!) and we cannot get away from the fact that they are a hybrid between the various types of a mixed breed of heavy horses.'

After the Clydesdale breed's foundation came a 60 year period when systematic breeding schemes were followed and the type fixed. The dates 1865 to 1925 approximately cover this period, and the first great sires were Darnley and Prince of Wales. Prince of Wales 673 was foaled in 1866, Darnley 222 in 1872. They were thus contemporaries for much of their working lives, and easily the most celebrated stallions of their day. Darnley was of misleading conformation. His photograph must be seen against a man to judge his true height, for his steeply sloping withers were deceiving. His sire was Conqueror 199, while his dam was the outstanding show mare Keir Peggy.

It is worth noting that these leading horses were no mere flashes in the pan. They were out of exceptionally good stock on both sides, even though a long list of shows and cups was not available for them to be proven. Keir Peggy's sire was Samson, alias Logan's Twin 741, foaled in 1855. He was a brown, and was bought by Sir William Stirling-Maxwell of Keir, Bart. Samson's sire was the dark brown Lofty 455, who won 1st Prize and Silver Medal at Glasgow. He travelled the Paisley district in 1854, Dalkeith in 1855 and Glasgow in 1856. He was by Farmer's Fancy 298, a bay foaled in 1841, who won first prize at the Highland Society's Glasgow Show in 1844. Second at the important Dumfries event of 1845, he travelled in Kintyre for many years.

This genealogical excursion is designed to show that the famous foundation stock did not just happen. Their breeders had followed the old concept of 'breed the best to the best, and hope for the best' and we can do little more in horse breeding today.

Darnley himself won the Glasgow Premium in 1876 and 1877, and the Highland Show championship in 1878 and 1884. For three years in succession he travelled the Stranraer district at the then enormous premium of 1,000 guineas, and was engaged on his fourth season when he died on September 30, 1886. Of Darnley's many sons, Top Gallant and the full brothers MacGregor and Flashwood were the best. Had Top Gallant done nothing more, he won claim to eternal fame as the sire of Sir Everard who in turn sired Baron's Pride (see below).

MacGregor, a bay with white hind feet, won the two progeny or group classes at the 1884 Highland Show. Sir Everard topped his class at the Glasgow Stallion Show five times. Among his sons was MacQueen, who with his offpring won at the Chicago livestock show before the turn of the century.

The dark brown Sir Everard was the right horse at the right time. Foaled in 1885, he was the grandson of Prince of Wales as well as of Darnley. Females from those two notable sires combined action with quality, yet tended to lack cart horse character. Sir Everard weighed 21 cwt in ordinary mature condition, standing no more than 17.1 hands. His girth measured 8 ft and his upper forearm

26 in round. Put to daughters of his two grandsires, he brought back much needed weight among his offspring. A Darnley granddaughter, Forest Queen, was the one destined for fame as mother of Baron's Pride, which she foaled to Sir Everard on May 7 1890.

Baron's Pride, a brown with white feet, was shown only once at the Highland Show when he was champion as a four-year-old for A. and W. Montgomery of Netherhall. The Montgomery family became the top exporters of Clydesdales up to World War 1. Though the horse did not himself win the Cawdor Cup, 11 of his offspring did. From 1896 he headed the list of winning sires, and regained the title in 1908 when he was 18. No wonder there were so many Baron's Pride offspring at the Carlisle Royal Show in 1902!

At the 1899 Highland Show, Baron's Pride offspring won over half the prizes. Eight daughters in the yearling filly class stood first, second, third, fourth, fifth, sixth, seventh and eighth. Legend recalls Baron's Pride's price as £400 when A. and W. Montgomery bought him along with another — and told the vendor to keep the other. The horse was limited to 90 or 100 mares a season and lived actively until 22.

Of Baron's Pride's many great breeding sons, the most successful was the brown Baron of Buchlyvie. He sired six Cawdor Cup winners and replaced his sire as the top breeding horse in Scotland. He was bought for £700, plus a gelding for luck, jointly by James Kilpatrick of Craigie Mains and William Dunlop of Dunure. The attraction was the very fine quality of bone and hair, and the horse improved as he matured, far exceeding his early promise.

It was said that Dunlop bought out his partner Kilpatrick for £2,000, but the precise nature of the transaction became the basis of an expensive law suit. The High Court first decided in favour of James Kilpatrick, then for Dunlop, and eventually the House of Lords agreed that the original decision with the horse as joint property was correct. The partnership had to be dissolved. A sale of the great horse took place on December 14 1911, and it is doubtful if there has ever been such a gathering of heavy horse people before or since. An agent acted for Dunlop and bought the Baron for £9,500.

This celebrated stallion had earned an estimated £2,000 to £3,000 for his owner in stud fees when a tragedy happened. The Baron was kicked on the foreleg by a mare and had to be put down. He was buried, but the skeleton was exhumed and is now on display in the Glasgow Museum. The broken bone shows clearly, and the exhibit is well worth a visit by every heavy horse lover. For demonstrating the structure of a draught horse it is incomparable.

James Kilpatrick tells the lawsuit story in *My 70 Years with Clydesdales*. Obviously he is telling his own side of the story, but he does compliment William Dunlop on his methods in breeding the best known Clydesdale of all time, Dunure Footprint. Foaled in 1908, he died in 1930, and in the years between made a fortune for his owner. Regrettably Dunlop entered the business life of Glasgow and lost his money, but Footprint at the height of his powers brought in £60 for each mare he served and £120 for every one he got in foal, which was a groom's yearly wage at the time. In two years the horse was credited with £15,000 in stud fees. In the Clydesdale Stud Book, Volume 39, 1917, 146 of his foals are registered. Taking into account mares not fruitful and those with dead or unregistered foals, it is easy to concede that Footprint did indeed serve the 300 mares per season claimed for him.

During the season he served a mare every two hours, day and night, 24 hours a day. Two cows were kept to supply him with milk, he ate huge quantities of eggs, and Richard Mitchell, a close friend of Footprint's groom, told me that after each service the great horse would collapse, legs spread-eagled in his box, until the next mare arrived. It does seem that these services were genuine. In other breeds and classes of stock substitutes have been introduced to ease the strain on expensive sires, but each mare's groom stayed with her when she visited Footprint, and not one of that dedicated race would see his master fobbed off with a horse other than the legendary stallion on his favourite mare.

William Dunlop reserved the right to buy back any colt foal of his choice for £300, and James Kilpatrick claims that Dunure Footprint left more foals in his lifetime than any other horse that ever lived.

Dunure Footprint started his showyard career as a foal, winning at Kilmarnock in 1908. He won the Cawdor Cup and the Brydon Shield, and was three times first and once second at the Royal Highland Show, but never won the championship there.

All modern Clydesdales are said to be traceable back to this famous stallion, and the roan which so affected the breed's colour in the 1960s and '70s is regarded as a Footprint influence. Certainly after his early years he was never photographed from his near side, on which he had a large light splatch. He was always posed with his head to the right of the photograph!

There is an inconsistency about his pedigree. His dam Dunure Ideal was originally entered in the stud book as by Baron of Buchlyvie, but when she produced Footprint as a son of Baron of Buchlyvie she was then entered as being sired by Auchenflower. There were no blood tests in those days! A groom who knew the line well asserted that the mare's hind leg conformation was such that she could only be by 'The Baron'. Such observations, while inconclusive, come from men who spent their whole lives with their stock and are not to be dismissed lightly. If this and other evidence be true, Baron of Buchlyvie was both Dunure Footprint's sire and his grandsire. That is evidently what James Kilpatrick thought when he wrote: 'Mr Dunlop experimented in some degree with in-breeding or line-breeding and it is my personal opinion that this was one of his successful experiments and had a lot to do with Footprint's phenomenal success as a breeder'.

My own Dunure Footprint story is melancholy and negative. I approached a Glasgow journalist for old heavy horse records. He told me how, when they were moving offices, he threw out a whole drawerful of Dunure stud cards!

OTHER FAMOUS STALLIONS

Bonnie Buchlyvie, foaled 1906, was another of 'The Baron's' many famous sons. A bay with his near legs white, he won the Cawdor Cup in 1909, and was sold to

James Kilpatrick in 1915 for 5,000 guineas. A grandson via Craigie McQuaid was Beau Ideal, claimed by James Kilpatrick as the best breeding stallion he ever owned. Beau Ideal was foaled in 1929 and lived for ten years. He and his most successful breeding son Craigie Chieftain were out of Dunure Footprint mares. A Footprint son, Kismet, was a black with face and legs white, and won the Cawdor Cup in 1917. His dam was the Baron's Pride mare Moira, showing how the thread of these wonderful sires runs through and through the Clydesdale breed.

A great-great grandson of Dunure Footprint was the bay Craigie Supreme Commander, winner of the 1947 Cawdor Cup and Supreme Champion again at Glasgow in 1952. His son Craigie Commodore won every major trophy, including the 1950 Cawdor Cup. Craigie Commodore's dam was by Craigie Beau Ideal and his granddam by Dunure Footprint, and he sired five Cawdor Cup winners and Callan's Favourite, who did well on the North American show circuit. The lighter colours that characterised the Clydesdale breed after World War 2 may be seen creeping in, for Craigie Commodore is described in Volume 71 of the stud book as: 'Bay; stripe on face, legs, spot on near side, splatch on off side and underbody white. Foaled 15th April, 1947. Owner James Kilpatrick, Craigie Mains, Kilmarnock, Ayrshire.'

Best known of all was Craigie Gallant Hero. Sire of three Cawdor Cup winners after taking it himself in 1960, he was sold for 2,600 guineas at the Craigie Mains dispersal in 1961.

THE PRINCE OF WALES LINE

Darnley and Prince of Wales were out of half-sisters. David Riddell, who bred Prince of Wales in 1866, sold him to Lawrence Drew for £1,500 as a five-year-old. When aged 18 the great horse was bought back by David Riddell at the Merryton dispersal for £945. So from 1884 to 1886 when Darnley died, Riddell owned both these classical stallions. Inter-breeding between the two lines 'nicked' and proved a great success.

Sons of Prince of Wales bred particularly well to Darnley daughters. The first-ever Cawdor Cup winners, Prince Alexander in 1892, and Prince of Kyle in 1893, were bred in that way. Kyle had a full brother, Prince of Albion, who was sold as a two-year-old for £3,000. The year was 1888, and Kyle became the first of 21 Cawdor Cup Winners for the Kilpatricks of Craigie Mains. A large number of Prince of Wales sons went to North America. Cedric, owned by Robert Holloaway in Illinois, was so successful that A. and W. Montgomery brought back to Scotland at least 14 sons and six daughters. One of the latter, Fickle Fortune Princess II, when mated to Baron's Pride produced the 1903 Cawdor Cup winner in Cedric Princess.

Hiawatha was a grandson of Prince of Wales, who perpetuated his line, winning the Cawdor Cup in four years out of five from 1898 to 1902, the Glasgow show not being held in 1900. He was a tall horse, a point he passed on, and sired three Cawdor Cup winners. Apukwa and Hiawatha Again were his most successful sons, the former standing second only to Dunure Footprint as the top Clydesdale breeder for several years, and he sired both Cawdor Cup winners in 1915.

Kilpatrick described Hiawatha as a slow maturer. As a young horse he was rather leggy, but developed into a great weighty stallion with beautiful limbs. His best known daughter was Boquhan Lady Peggy, and, said Kilpatrick, 'the Clydesdale breed was fortunate at that time to have three such outstanding sires of different breeding — Baron's Pride to perpetuate the Darnley strain, Hiawatha the Prince of Wales strain, and Royal Favourite a blend of both'.

A GREAT SHOW RECORD

Fyvie Sensation, foaled in 1918, was by Hiawatha Again out of a Dunure Footprint mare, Lady Ivo. Her full sister Farleton Lady Alice won the Cawdor Cup in 1921, and their dam was an Everlasting mare. Fyvie Sensation had a tremendous show career, but his greatest claim to fame is as the sire of Benefactor.

The photograph of Benefactor is regarded by *Scottish Farmer* photographer and Clydesdale Horse Society Secretary John Fraser as the finest ever taken of the breed. Benefactor was foaled in 1922, and like his sire was out of a Dunure Footprint mare. He won every major award including the Cawdor Cup in 1925, and sired seven winners of it. The intertwining pedigrees of these famous Clydesdales from the mid-1860s until the 1920s are worthy of careful study by breeders of any class of stock.

Benefactor was sold for 4,400 guineas as a three-year-old and succeeded Dunure Footprint as Scotland's top breeding horse. Unfortunately he died young, aged ten.

Attention being lavished on a young Clydesdale at the Royal Highland (Audrey Hart).

Left *Clydesdale geldings Duke and Pete, owned by Mr Tom Brewster of Bandirran, Fife.*

Right *The prize-winning Clydesdale mare Stainsby Dawn and her colt foal Alfie, bred in North Yorkshire.*

Bottom right *A pair of Clydesdales, nicely decorated in the southern style, driven by Harold Sherfield (Colin Fry).*

His line continued through Golden Dawn, foaled in 1947, a roan with four white legs, and a grey fore ankle. He was owned by John Young, then of West Doura, Kilwinning. Golden Dawn sired Lorna Doone, dam of Craigie Gallant Hero, and Doura Perfection, foaled in 1955. He became the top breeding horse of the early 1960s, but both he and Dunsyre Benedictine succumbed to grass sickness in the spring of 1965.

Some Doura Perfection stock was exported to North America, two of them standing second and fourth at the 1966 Royal Winter Fair. First and third places were taken by Bardhill Castle offspring, that horse having been imported by Canadian Wreford Hewson. Bardhill Castle suffered an injury soon after arriving, effectively ending his show career, but through his stock he became the leading breeding horse in the North America of the 1960s.

Another successful export of the Benefactor line was Balwill Print, who sired two Cawdor Cup winners before he went to Australia, where he did an excellent job until he was in his twenties. Bardhill Vintage, who like his sire Glenord was out of a Dunure Footprint mare, was Grand Champion at the Canadian Royal, from 1969 to 1972, and again in 1975 for Anheuser-Busch.

One of Glenord's sons who stayed in Britain was an object of controversy through no fault of his own. Hayston Ideal sired the winning Bardrill Enterprise among many others, Enterprise going to the Gordeyko Brothers in Canada in 1976. Hayston Ideal passed from Scotland into England for a time under another name, and was registered as a Shire. This was before the official blood testing scheme was under way, but the horse's offspring were deleted from the Shire Horse Society stud book.

Torrs Benefactor, Torrs Renown and Doura Aristocrat represent three more generations of this Prince of Wales/Benefactor line. Doura Aristocrat won the

Clydesdales in winter clothing. The mare (right) is Kettleston Apple Blossom, many times a champion.

Cawdor Cup in 1970, and sired three winners of it before he left for Australia. One of these winners, in 1976, was Doura Masterstroke, who has himself also sired three Cawdor Cup winners.

So the well-founded lines persisted. A Scottish exile farming in Yorkshire said: 'What a pity the majority of Clydesdale breeders went off horses altogether when the heavy horse was disappearing from the land. Had they changed to bloodstock or ponies, they would surely have succeeded, for they were such skilled and dedicated horsemen.'

NORTHERN IRELAND

One place where those breeding skills remained was Northern Ireland. During the breed's heyday there were Clydesdale stallions travelling widely in Ireland and the Shire never gained a comparable foothold there. In the 1921 stud book of The Clydesdale Horse Society of the United Kingdom of Great Britain and Ireland, 47 Irish stallions were registered, mainly from Londonderry but also from Fermanagh, Antrim and Co Down. In 1936 there were 30 in Northern Ireland, and 46 in the then Irish Free State (Eire). The Isle of Man also had its quota.

Today activity is concentrated in the north, with a successful foal show at Ballymoney. Links with Scotland are strong, and judges at the 1983 show were Tom Brewster, Bandirran, Cupar, Fife, and his near neighbour Ronald Black, Fyvie. This Londonderry Horse Breeding Society event attracted 30 Clydesdales, including 12 colt foals and nine filly foals. Great names surfaced. The champion filly foal was by Johnston Aristocrat, and the reserve by Doura Masterstroke, who stood for two seasons. By Doura Aristocrat out of Barlauchlan Snowflake, Masterstroke followed his son Doura Winston, foaled in 1977 out of Sheddock Marianne, in the succession of top-class Clydesdale stallions hired by the Society.

In 1982 a Doura Winston daughter crossed the Irish Sea to become Supreme Champion at the Scottish Winter Fair, staged at Ingliston, Edinburgh. She stood reserve champion in Ireland, and her new owner Robert Kirkwood renamed her Drumlee Lady. She was top two-year-old filly at the 1984 Glasgow Stallion Show, and Female Champion. In 1985 she became the Cawdor Cup winner.

The Londonderry Society was founded after World War 2 by the late Senator Drennan, whose laudable aim was simply to improve the Clydesdale horse in Ulster. Then John Crowe and Wilson McCracken took over for 16 years, with the latter still an active organiser. He bred a notable colt by Doura Winston out of the double Royal Ulster winner Carfinton Lady Kathryn, that stood 17.1 hands high before he was two years old.

A proof of Northern Ireland quality is the frequency with which their Clydesdales are bought by Scottish breeders, who then after a brief show career re-export them to Canada and the USA. North American demand has certainly helped revive the Scottish breed, but I am by no means alone in wondering whether this constant draining of top blood is being overdone. In 1982, 22 Clydesdales left Scottish shores for Canada and the USA. The most notable was Craighead Clementine, Supreme Champion at the first Aberdeen Clydesdale Show, and bred by Quintin Macmorland, High Craighead, Girvan. Others to go that year included Barlauchlan Lady Luck and the sweet Yardfoot Athenia. Naturally foals take pride of place, the formidable air freight charge being based on weight.

The 1984 Cawdor Cup winner (male) was the tall, strikingly coloured Greendykes Royale, shown by James Young. The female award at the Royal Highland went deservedly to Kettlestoun Valetta, owned by Robert McDonald, and bred by the late Robert Lawrie out of his wonderful mare Apple Blossom. Robert Lawrie's success with cattle, sheep, ducks and Clydesdales demonstrated that large numbers are not an essential prerequisite of successful breeding.

James Young was again successful in 1985, when his yearling colt Greendykes Pioneer, bred by Jim McCulloch, took the top male honour from William Wilson's Cummertrees Criffel Commander. Also a yearling, Cummertrees Criffel Commander was by Doura Magnificent 'The Canadian Horse', so-called by Clydesdale men as James Young bought him from across the Atlantic.

THE STANDARD FOR CLYDESDALE HORSES

1 The head must be strong, intelligent and carried high. The forehead open, broad between the eyes, wide muzzle, large nostrils, bright clear eyes, big ears and a well arched long neck springing out of an oblique shoulder with high withers.

2 The body should be deep, the back short and the ribs well sprung. The kidneys should be below the level of the withers and the tail placed high but well set in.

Above *Foot dressing the Clydesdales* (Audrey Hart).

Below *Immaculate leg feathering on Clydesdales at the Scottish Winter Fair* (Audrey Hart).

More body white is allowed on the Clydesdale than on the Shire. The mare is Bandirran Bonnie, the foal by Johnston Aristocrat (Audrey Hart).

3 Mature stallions should be 17.1 to 18 hands and mares 16.3 to 17.2 hands.

4 The colour should be preferably bay or brown with a white stripe on the face, legs white over knees and hocks.

5 Forelegs must be planted well under the shoulders. There should be no openness at the knees or tendency to knock knees. Knees should be big and broad at the front. The cannon bones should be long to place the knee well up the leg. The ankles should be fine, of medium length and set at an angle of 45°. The foot should be large and strong, the hoof head wide and springy.

6 Hindlegs must be set close together with the hocks turned inwards. The thighs must come well down to the hocks, clean and well packed with muscle and sinew. The cannon bones again must be long. The hocks should be broad, clean and sharply developed. The ankles should be fine, of medium length and at a lesser angle than the fore ankles. The feet should be large and sound with a tendency to strength on the outside.

7 The bones should be broad and flat with an abundance of long silky hair hanging from behind the knees and from the hocks to the ground. The front of the bones should be clean but the hair should again spring from the hoof head to the ground.

8 The front action should be straight with the ankle and knee joints being well utilised. The hind action close, clear and defined.

9 The general appearance should be of strength, power and activity. Quality as well as quantity.

Chapter 6
The Suffolk horse

'Those remarkable features, the uniformity of colour, the short leg, the rounded carcasses, the longevity with vitality, frequently reaching nearly 30 years of age, are still the well-known characteristics of the Suffolk Horse.' Herman Biddell's words are as true today as when the first Secretary of the Suffolk Horse Society spoke them in 1907. The Suffolk is the oldest pure heavy horse breed in the British Isles, and though claims that every modern Suffolk is descended from the early Blake's Farmer are unfounded, there has been none of the crossing that took place between Shire and Clydesdale and no sign of the Arab blood that distinguishes the Percheron. Camden's Brittania dates the Suffolk back to at least 1506 AD. In the early 18th century there is mention of the breed in archaeological works on the county, and in the mid-18th century the Suffolk is listed as a pure breed.

The first and retrospective volumes of both the Clydesdale and Shire stud books are fascinating reading, with a wealth of detail on genealogical trees, but for scope and format Volume 1 of the Suffolk Stud Book, 1880, stands alone. It measures 12 in × 9 in and weighs over 6 lb. Its 712 pages contain a number of

Suffolk mare and foal bred by Mr Maurice Race, Barnard Castle, County Durham.

extended pedigrees. It lists Suffolk shades of chesnut, in this breed always spelt without the central 't', which are the same in the 1980s.

There are seven shades — the dark, at times approaching a brown-black, mahogany or liver colour, the dull dark chesnut, the light mealy chesnut, the red, the golden, the lemon, and the bright chesnut. The most popular, the most common and the most standing colour is the last named. The bright chesnut is a lively colour with a little graduation of lighter colour at the flanks and at the extremities — but not too much. It is, in most cases, attended by a star on the forehead, or thin 'reach', 'blaze', or 'shim' down the face. The flaxen mane and tail prevalent a hundred years ago (ie, around 1778) are usually seen in the light chesnut.

Colours are registered by the breeder, and may not always be accurate, as a 1983 example shows. Blaxhall Bruce was described as a 'whole coloured light chesnut' when he was foaled on June 4 1979. By the time he was four he was a red chesnut. No reflection is intended on the truth or correctness of these registrations but they show how the shade of chesnut may change with the years.

HERMAN BIDDELL

Of all the dedicated, enthusiastic, hard-working and unbiased breed society secretaries who have graced the British livestock industry, few have been the peer of Herman Biddell and none has excelled him. His industry and accuracy leap from the pages of that gigantic first stud book.

Relevant known details of each entry are listed, some going back many years. Opening the work at random, I found Proctor 66, a red chesnut foaled in 1824. He was bred by Mr Barker, sired by Barker's Bay Proctor 65, bred by Kersey, and out of a mare by Thurkettle's Proctor 1195, granddam of the Shadingfield stock. Biddell writes of Proctor 66:

> A real Shadingfield bred horse with white hind legs; his sire, dam and granddam all being of that stock. This is the horse that Barker gave to his old servant Woolnough; who sold him to Mr Shorten, of Ipswich. From his hands he passed into those of Mr David Dowsett, a dealer in Essex, from whom he was purchased for the sum of 400 guineas for His Majesty William IV. Moyse described him as 'a sweet pretty horse, a dark chesnut with white hind legs'. He was sire of G. Gooch's 598, Greenard's 623, and a number of other Proctors. Through Barthropp's Hero 88 and his descendants, we still have a strain of the Shadingfield stock at the present day [1880]: the sire of Hero 88, Wilson's Goliath 1317, came of a mare by Barker's Chesnut Proctor 66, but there is little of the characteristic of the blood in any of his progeny.

Some have more and some less detail. Hero 88 (mentioned above) was 'a red chesnut horse of great muscular development, and big legs'. Besides a number of registered stallions, his offspring included 'a number of wide-framed mares with the best legs and good colour'. Cup-bearer III 566 was among his descendants. The excellent detail in his portrait justifies the high praise Biddell heaped on the artist, Duvall of Ipswich:

It is easy enough to give an outline; and with a bald face, three white legs, and some unmistakable colour, to call the picture a portrait. But Mr Duvall has had to deal with very different material. To produce individuality of character in the portrait of a Suffolk horse, requires no little practice; the rotundity of form; the absence of anatomical development, and the extraordinary similarity of likeness, renders the task one of extreme difficulty. The value of these portraits — especially those of the mares — as historical records of the present day will, in after years be far above and beyond the performances of those 'animal painters' who, not claiming to be called artists, cover the walls of the harness house with impossible portraits of celebrated horses.

Biddell would have been properly contemptuous of those modern artists who have preferred to jump on the heavy horse band wagon before they studied equine anatomy. Even the Shire on the postage stamp which was issued in 1978 looked half a Clydesdale!

Biddell did not shirk from derogatory references, nor did the Suffolk Horse Society from printing them. Boxer 335 was 'a plain colt with great hindquarters'. Duke 357, bred by Mr Crisp, 'had bad feet'. Farmers' Glory 458 was sold in 1812 for £10. 'He was then in bad condition,' says one who saw him, 'lousy, but turned out a good horse.'

A big man in every respect, Biddell stood 6 ft 4 in tall and weighed 19 stone. He was quickly called on by one of the joint secretaries of the Suffolk Stud Book Association, formed in 1877, to compile a retrospective register of genuine Suffolk stallions. Having been deeply interested in the matter for 15 years, it took Biddell a further three to trace 1,236 stallions spanning 120 years. He worked alone, gave up politics, had no time to practice his artist's skills and did not properly oversee his farm — and a farm is a hard task master. According to Keith Chivers, the churchwardenship of St Mary's, Playford, was the only duty he did not neglect during these historical labours. 'He was sole warden for 44 years but, when the vicar began to point out that the law required two, he regarded the idea as preposterous, and resigned. It was a waste of time for two men to do what one could manage equally well.'

In 1917 Herman Biddell died, having retired from active farming a quarter of a century before. He retained his vigorous opinions to the end, waxing outrageously about 'daylight saving' introduced during World War 1. His work remains a model for anyone whose good fortune it is to belong to the livestock world. His successor as Secretary of the Suffolk Horse Society was Fred Smith, who wrote of him: 'It was in March, 1917, that Mr Biddell, full of years, passed away and was laid to rest in the parish of Playford — near the white farm house on the brow of the hill, and the grey old hall in the valley below — where his life had been spent. All honour to his name.'

DEVELOPMENT OF THE BREED

It is instructive to recall that the Suffolk was a distinct breed when now fertile east

Suffolk was mainly heath, before swedes and mangels were widely grown or modern sheep breeds established. The old Norfolk Horn sheep held sway, cattle required four or five years to fatten, and a hooded waggon with six horses was the means by which ordinary people travelled from Saxmundham to London, which they rarely did.

That was in the late 18th century, and in the early 19th the Suffolk horse was gaining ground and improving from the type Northumberland farmer George Culley referred to in *Observations on Live Stock*, 1794: 'It is probable their merit consists more in constitutional hardiness than true shape [he remembered seeing few above $15^1/_2$ hands high] being in general a very plain made horse; their colour mostly yellowish or sorrel, with a white ratch or blaze on their faces; the head large, ears wide, muzzle coarse, fore-end low, back long, but very straight, sides flat, shoulders too far forward, hind quarters middling, but rather high about the hips, legs round and short in the pasterns, deep bellied, and full in the flank.' Even allowing for any regional bias, George Gulley's description does not bring to mind a horse of great beauty of form. He acknowledges, however, that 'these horses do perform a surprising day's work; it is well known that the Suffolk and Norfolk farmers plough more land in a day than any other people in the island, and these are the kind of horses everywhere used in those districts. Even today Roger and Cheryl Clark of Weylands Farm, Stoke-by-Nayland have proved that 'you can work your show horses and show your work horses'.

The longer and harder day's work of which the Suffolk was capable may be due to the 'deep bellied' characteristic to which Culley referred. 'We know from observation and experience that all deep-bellied horses carry their food long', said the writer. The common East Anglian practice was to work one long shift in the field, rather than spend time returning home for the midday meal.

A Suffolk stallion and a few mares were introduced into Scotland by the Earl of Hopetoun. His Lordship's groom informed Culley that both they and their progeny answered very well, but they were not established north of the Border. The Earl was, apparently, one of those now so often derided landed gentry who, said Culley, 'is never so happy as when he can introduce anything that will benefit his tenants, neighbours and country'. Today, however, Aberdeen City Council keeps three among its Clydesdales, and one broke its 500-mile journey from Suffolk in our Borders stable.

Early in the 19th century three great men dominated the Suffolk horse world. Catlin was a frequent show winner, as was Crisp, who spread his Butley Abbey stock far and wide, while Barthropp painstakingly maintained the breed character. Thomas Crisp of Butley was grandson of the Thomas Crisp of Ufford, who bred the famous 'Crisp's Horse of Ufford', whose genes were found in most of the thousands of Suffolk horses throughout the world in their heyday. The younger Thomas took over the farm of 800 acres at Gedgrave Hall when aged only 19, on the death of his father.

Thomas Crisp soon mastered the running of so large a concern, and made his mark as a livestock breeder also. Later he moved to Butley Abbey, where he bred Shorthorn cattle and Southdown sheep. He was one of those universal breeders who enliven the farming scene from time to time — men who succeed with every class of stock to which they turn their hand. Thomas Crisp excelled with Small White, Berkshire, and an improved Butley type of Black Suffolk Pig. For 30 years after 1837 he may well have won more prizes than any other man in the same space of time, before or since. He did not wait for late 20th century transport to compete on the Continent. He won at Paris, Stettin and Hamburg, and shipped trainloads of stock abroad.

The outward looking exploits of such an individual have markedly beneficial and stimulating effects on other stockbreeders. The contrary was proved in the 1970s when some office holders in the Suffolk Horse Society opposed exports on the grounds that damage would be done to the pitifully small nucleus remaining at home. A more enlightened outlook in the 1980s found new markets overseas so successfully that every possible mare was put to the stallion, when previously the stimulus of a remunerative market had been lacking.

One may imagine the pleasant rumours circulating the countryside in Crisp's day when he gained an order from a German Baron for six two-year-olds of one colour, and so was buying up every decent colt likely to fit the bill. That was the age at which he said of his great horse Cupbearer, 'Whoever lives to see him, that will make the best horse I ever had'.

Among notable early exports was a Suffolk stallion purchased by Mr C. G. Tindall, at the Royal Show in 1856. Mr Tindall was engaged in heavy transport work in Australia, where his teams often covered several hundreds of miles along no more than a beaten track. He claimed three virtues for the Suffolk and its crosses. They withstood the heat well. They could lie on the road and, by simply grazing the waysides, frequently ended a journey in better condition than they began it. Most importantly, they made an excellent cross on the native mares.

EARLY CHARACTERISTICS

The two chief characteristics claimed by early Suffolk Horse Society secretaries on behalf of their breed were endurance and constitution. A young breeder found himself as a transport driver in France during World War I, and remarked that at home he had heard much about feet and legs, but when actually working one himself he preferred one with good girth, well ribbed up and hardy constitution. The Suffolk of the day fulfilled these qualifications admirably. 'A good performer at his work and a keen performer at the manger, always carrying a fair proportion of flesh, whether the rations be scant or plentiful', is claimed in an early breed history.

It has been said that the Suffolk's predisposition to breed only chesnuts, and no other colour, is proof of its pure breeding and antiquity. Modern genetics lend a more simple answer. If the chesnut colour is recessive, and two recessives are mated together, the resulting colour cannot be other than chesnut. The 'purity' of the breed is best shown by the similarity of type right down the years since the first photographs were taken. A Shire or Clydesdale photograph may be dated to within a decade or so simply by looking at the horse; with the Suffolk this is seldom possible.

Modern Suffolk conformation is remarkably like that of almost a century ago. This is Wedgwood 1749, Champion Stallion at the Windsor Royal Show in 1889.

Another aspect is longevity. At an early Suffolk Agricultural Association show, a mare was exhibited with a suckling filly by her side. The filly was two years old but, according to reliable evidence at the time, the mare was 37 years old at the time of foaling!

At Leeds in 1861, the first prize horse was Webb's Rising Star 1266, and his dam was 22 years old when he was foaled. The horse appears in Volume 1 of the Suffolk Stud Book, the details being supplied by Herman Biddell, so may be taken as fact. Rising Star was bred in 1855 by Mr Jonas Webb at Babraham, Cambridgeshire, still a vital name in stock breeding circles through its Agricultural Research Council establishment. The dam was bought at the Eyke Rookery sale as a young mare, and was in good working order when she was rising 27.

In the Registry of Mares, Volume 1, 1880, Lofft has 37 mares. Barthropp's and Crisp's blood is among them, and many were foaled in the 1870s. Biddell lists four generations of Suffolks which spanned 73 years, the average age of three of the four being over 30. Brag, foaled in 1851, was still alive aged 28 when her breeder, Samuel Stanford, passed on details of her breeding to the stud book editor. 'Her dam, Depple, was shot when she was rising 33 years. She was a

Punch.

daughter of Mr Thomas Johnson's first Boxer 747, of Leiston, and he was a son of Julian's famous bung-tailed Boxer 755, who was foaled about 1805. Julian's Boxer travelled 25 seasons, and died when he was something over 30 years old.'

The Reverend O. Reynolds of Debach owned another notable mid-19th century Suffolk dam. Diamond 591 was by Albert 507, who won at the Royal Show in Gloucester in 1853. She was one of 16 foals which the Reverend O. Reynolds bred from her dam in successive years, which he bought as a two-year-old at the Quay Horse Repository, Ipswich. One may imagine the delight with which Diamond's maternal feats were welcomed at the rectory each spring. To buy a two-year-old at a repository sale and find such a treasure is the kind of good fortune that stock breeders dream about.

Diamond bred several notable foals, including Lofft's Cupbearer 824. Crisp's Blyth 1072, first as a foal at Framlingham, and Colonel Wilson's Cupbearer 1294, were others. The mare was bought by Mr Crisp of Butley Abbey, then at the famous Butley Abbey sale of 1870 she was bought by Mr Lofft, and in 1880 was still at the Troston Hall stud. Lofft's Cupbearer 842 was a large, heavy, short-legged horse, very dark in colour. His owner held an annual sale at Troston Hall, and was a breeder of considerable note, with six stallions entered in Volume 1, with notable prizes amongst them.

SOCIETY MARES

In 1900 the Suffolk Horse Society made one of its periodic flights of practical imagination, and initiated a scheme for Society Mares. It agreed to supply to a limited number of small-scale tenant farmers a Suffolk mare for breeding purposes.

After being selected, the applicant could purchase any mare approved by the Society at its Annual Autumn Sale, to a price limit of 60 guineas. The tenant farmer agreed to pay a minimum 25 per cent of the purchase money at the close of the sale, the balance being paid by the Society. The farmer paid interest to the Society at four per cent, and a free service was made by a nomination stallion. The foal was to be delivered to the Society show and sale at Ipswich, and the breeder received a guaranteed £16 10s for the foal, which then became the property of the Society. All such foals were then put up for unreserved sale, the breeders being allowed to bid and purchase on the same terms as anyone else. The breeder received half of any sum over 20 guineas.

The nomination stallions referred to were purchased annually by the Society, authority for 30 being decided in 1897. A Committee was set up, with the dual objectives of encouraging the breeding of good Suffolk horses and assisting small farmers, ie, those under 200 acres. This Committee met early in January and selected stallions for which nominations would be purchased. They paid attention to the locality in which the stallions would travel, pre-empting the Race Horse Betting Levy Board's admirable Premium Stallion Scheme by some 70 years.

In the 1912 stud book came the first news of a Board of Agriculture list of approved stallions. Only four names were entered in the first list, which covered three months up to February 29 1912, and none of them is particularly well known. A 'Veterinary' appointed by the Board had passed them as free from hereditary disease. In the next stud book to October 31 1913, matters were under way, and 40 were registered. To these were added a further 26, up to January 31 1914.

GROOMS

Secretary Fred Smith had a pleasant turn of phrase and his obituaries depicted men typical of those who have served the British livestock industry so well for so long. In Volume 17, 1910, he wrote:

Among Suffolk grooms, truly the old order has passed away, and the familiar Showyard figures of the two Lancasters, and John Burrows, will be seen no more amongst us. No more loyal type of man could be found than these three veterans. They were loyal to their masters, loyal to their horses, and loyal to their fellow workers, and thus set an example to those who in other spheres of life are engaged in similar competitions; for through all their efforts to secure foremost place, not a single point against their horse or their master was allowed to go unchallenged. At the same time they were ever ready to recognise the ability of others and to congratulate the successful exhibitor. Fortunately there are those in the present generation of grooms who, stepping into the old places, will take a pride in handing on the honourable traditions of the profession to their successors.

In 1924 Fred Smith retired after almost 40 years' tenure of the Secretary's office. He was thus only the second in nearly half a century. Five years previously Wilf Woods had become Assistant Secretary, a post in which he remained until 1966, when he took over the Secretaryship. A gentle, attentive and kindly man, he gave almost his whole life to the welfare of the Suffolk horse and its breeders, and lived to see the revival of the late 1970s.

THE GREAT WAR AND AFTER

The Suffolk did not have the same capabilities as the biggest Shires and Clydesdales as a city dray horse. Its weight did not match the really heavy loads, and it remained steadfast to its original purpose as an agricultural horse. The clean legs looked somewhat insubstantial to eyes accustomed to clouds of feather, although careful bone measurements showed that appearances were often deceptive in this respect.

Its clean legs and sound constitution were an asset, however, in the dreadful and unforseeable conditions of World War 1. A few months before that war ended, the Sudbourne stud was dispersed after the death of its owner, Mr Kenneth Clark, to meet prices that were then a record at public auction. Sudbourne Beau Brocade, a five-year-old stallion, and the filly Sudbourne Moonlight two years younger, each realised 2,000 guineas. This was a tremendous sale, with 98 animals averaging £338 11s 6d, even though 17 foals were included. Another Sudbourne stallion figured in a further record, when in 1920 the two-year-old Sudbourne Foch was bought by the Army Authorities for 2,200 guineas. The British Army was at that time buying Suffolks for artillery and transport work.

The 1920s proved a desperate decade for British agriculture, and arable farming in the Eastern Counties suffered so badly that many farms were unlet and improvements out of the question. Suffolk horse trade inevitably suffered in the general depression, though an export trade remained. Despite poor farm prices, Suffolk breeders made a huge effort to back their native breeds when the Royal Show was staged in Ipswich in 1934. The parade of over 300 chesnuts made a memorable day.

Though the depression continued until the outbreak of World War 2 in 1939, Suffolk breeders gained some cheer from the formation of a Royal stud at Sandringham in 1937, for King George VI. His father, King George V, had been a great supporter of the heavy horse and a dedicated Shire breeder.

Eastern Counties farmers were in the forefront of mechanisation after World War 2, and Suffolk horse numbers plummeted. Some pure-bred studs withstood the great slaughter of the late 1940s and early 1950s, but by 1960 the remaining animals were growing old. Secretary Wilfred Woods later reckoned that their worst period was just beginning. The Society then met to consider its future. The President, Colonel Sir Robert E. S. Gooch, thought that with economical management they could last another 12 years. Well before those years had

Suffolk and geese in Nottinghamshire (Audrey Hart).

passed, the outlook brightened ever so slightly.

By 1970 there was a sprinkling of new breeders, and when Charlie Saunders held his reduction sale in October 1974 a Suffolk gelding sold for 500 guineas. A mare realised 1,450 guineas and a filly foal 1,350 guineas. A year later on the death of George E. Colson the Rowhedge dispersal brought buyers from as far afield as County Durham and Hampshire, with a stallion making 900 guineas, a mare 920 guineas, and a filly foal 1,000 guineas.

1977 was the centenary of the Suffolk horse, a head in front of both Shire and Clydesdale. The year concluded with a dinner at which the still sprightly Wilfred Woods was honoured by his President Colonel Gooch, the event being attended by the Presidents of the British Percheron and Shire Horse Societies. It is worth repeating that one of the pleasantest aspects of the heavy horse's renaissance is the accord and friendship among all its members, and the absence of inter-breed emnities and jealousies which were once such an unpleasant feature of the scene.

Following the death of Colonel Sir Robert Gooch, the Benacre stud was dispersed in 1979 and its undoubted breeding spread throughout the Suffolk world.

THE CLARKS AND THE COLONY

A tragic happening which the breed did not deserve was the death through lightning of Rowhedge Count II, a stallion who for conformation, size and temperament was a tremendous asset, very successful as a breeder, while in the show ring he gained many prizes for Roger and Cheryl Clark. Count led the parade of Ipswich Town after their FA Cup Final victory in 1977, and paraded at the Wembley Horse of the Year Show, in 1977. Roger has so popularised the

Young Suffolks at Hollesley Bay Colony (Audrey Hart).

Suffolk breed that he was made the first Chairman of the Suffolk Horse Society, and is a Fellow and Liveryman of the Worshipful Company of Farriers and a Freeman of the City of London. His wife Cheryl is an accomplished farrier and the pair take in a number of horses of several breeds for breaking and foaling.

Mention must be made of the sterling work done by HM Hollesley Bay Colony, a Borstal institution where many wayward youngsters have found new purpose in life when in charge of the big Suffolks. Estate manager John Bramley ensured that the Suffolks play an active part in the work of the 1,400 acres estate, and the sight of the long stable with its row of spotless stalls is fascinating to heavy horse people, while the quality of Colony blood helps the breed at large.

Suffolks are now spreading into the West Country. A happy aspect is that most of the horses there are working and proving economic on smaller farms and steep hillsides.

SOUND FEET

The Suffolk was once condemned for bad feet. This is now difficult to believe, for the breed can claim parity with any other for soundness, and its devotees believe it to be superior. Realising that the problem existed, the breed society instituted Foot Classes between the Wars at the main shows. The practice continues, and a practising farrier or veterinary surgeon is always called upon to judge. One of them, Hector Moore of Brandestone, shod Suffolks before World War 2. 'If ever I find an unsound foot, I think,"This takes me back to the old days. Feet like these used to be far more common,"' he said. 'The earlier Suffolks had a much flatter foot, and dropped soles and sandcracks were common faults, and the main reason for introducing classes.'

Hector Moore said that the soundest horn is grainy and stripey, like a piece of marble. A blue hoof is different in texture from white. Shape is very important, for if the foot tends to go under at the heel, it is a sign of sidebones which are not yet showing. He recounted an East Anglian custom that grew up around a young horse's first shoeing. A gallon of beer was presented for every shoe, and if there were several smiths at the smithy, they would each shoe one foot. If their first nail was not driven in straight, they forfeited the beer.

Allied to skilled farriery, breeding from sound footed horses and the impetus of show classes has been better stable management, including sound drainage, which has helped to eradicate most foot problems.

EXPORTS

Overseas sales have acted as leaven to the Suffolk breed ever since the Society was formed in 1877. Not all went smoothly. Diadem 1553 left a string of home winners before 1899 but was sold to Canada, only to break his neck on the journey. He was a great-grandson of Cupbearer 2nd 542. Benbow 1598 was re-sold by Galbraiths 'to go among the Mormons, where he will doubtless help to spread the stock of the big-boned Ben 139 in the far West.' Other Suffolks at the turn of the century were sold to Buenos Aires, Nebraska and Iowa, while Gold Dust 1824 won the sweepstake prize at the Oregon spring show in 1889 for any age or breed.

In the 1900 stud book, 23 export certificates were registered. By 1910 this had risen to 129, and just before World War 1 173 certificates were granted, while doubtless more were exported with no certificate. The 1920 stud book registered no exports, through difficulties of transport. In the 1930s, Suffolks were exported to Canada, the USA, Chile, Argentina, and South Africa, the biggest consignment of 14 stallions and 62 mares going to the USA in 1938. In 1955 and 1956 the Pakistan government chose Suffolks for pure breeding and mule breeding, and imported three stallions and 47 mares. These were followed by 16 mares in the next two years, and a stallion in 1977.

The early 1980s saw another flurry of interest, which could have continuous effect on home breeding. American heavy horse enthusiasts found the Suffolk to their liking and have bought the colt Marshland Appollo from Ivan Cooke, Great Yarmouth, following the deep red chesnut Marshland Punch, rising two. Roger and Cheryl Clark and Philip Almy have also supplied young horses, and the reaction has proved most encouraging. Jutland has bought a Suffolk stallion to introduce new blood to their breed.

SCALE OF POINTS FOR SUFFOLK HORSES
As printed in Volume 27 of the Suffolk Stud Book, 1935

Points

Colour Chesnut; a star, a little white on face, or a few silver hairs is no
detriment.   } 25
Head Big with broad forehead.

Neck Deep in collar tapering gracefully towards the setting of the head.
Shoulders Long and muscular,well thrown back at the withers.   } 50

Carcass Deep round ribbed from shoulder to flank, with graceful outline in
back, loin, and hindquarters; wide in front and behind (the tail well up, with
good second thighs).

Feet, joints and legs The leg should be straight with fair sloping pasterns, big
knees and long clean hocks on short cannon bones free from coarse hair.
Elbows turn in regarded as a serious defect. Feet having plenty of size, with
circular form protecting the frog.   20

Walk Smart and true.

Trot Well balanced all round with good action.   } 5

                                                                          100

Chapter 7
The Percheron

After the Boer War a Royal Commission on horse breeding was appointed. It found that 90 per cent of London bus horses were bought in America, or at Liverpool after landing from that country. Lieutenant Colonel Sir Merrick Burrell, Bart, CBE, Inspector of Remounts 1915-18, said that these horses were undoubtedly the produce of Percheron sires on the American farmers' working mares. Many were purchased from the omnibus companies to horse the artillery in the South African War and proved the greatest success.

No peacetime army depending on horse transport can maintain its needs for war. The extra horses must come from 'Civvy Street', and that is what happened when World War 1 broke out. Demand for light draught horses and for very active, hardy and heavy draught horses increased daily, and out of all proportion to that for other types. The United Kingdom simply could not provide sufficient. In 1914 a Remount Purchasing Commission, including many of the best known judges in Great Britain, visited Canada and the USA. According to Lieutenant Colonel Merrick Burrell, horses showing strong Percheron characteristics proved the most suitable. The Commission noted the uniformity of Percheron-bred stock from the nondescript mares of the country, a theme repeated throughout this chapter. The Percherons were also reported as 'wonderfully good tempered', withstanding long journeys by rail and sea better than others.

In 1916 Sir William Birbeck, Director of Remounts, sent Colonel T.R.F. Bate, Royal Artillery, and Lieutenant-Colonel Sir Merrick Burrell to compare the various breeds of draught horse at the French Government Haras (stud farm). They and the officer there all agreed that they preferred the Percheron to all other types. Sir William concluded that the civilian population should breed and use a hardier, more active and cleaner-legged draught horse than it was doing.

The English Ministry of Agriculture took up this point from Sir William, and arranged with the French Ministry for the export of two pure-bred Percheron stallions and 12 mares. Lord Lonsdale and Mr Henry Overman agreed to purchase them to start the experiment. A further Commission of highly competent horsemen selected and purchased more animals in 1917. In 1920, 45 Percheron mares and fillies were imported and sold to home breeders. Thus the French breed's importation into Britain was done in no haphazard manner. Those responsible did not seek financial gain, nor to harm the native British breeds.

Percheron.

Their sole aim was to introduce a heavy draught breed of great activity; one that could be bred and used profitably during peace time, yet when mated with lighter mares would produce light draught horses suitable for army purposes.

The Minister of Agriculture, Lord Ernie, told a deputation of English horse breeders that the country's need was for a heavy horse that could trot. In a foreword to a book *The Horse and War* by Captain Sydney Galtrey, Field Marshal Lord Haig wrote: 'I hope it will be brought home to the people of the British Empire the wisdom of breeding animals with the two military virtues of hardiness and activity, and I would add that the best animals for army purposes are also the most valuable for agriculture, commerce and sport'.

The British Percheron Horse Society was formed in 1918. Its aim was to look after the interests, control the breeding of the animals, and form a stud book into which should be entered all those pure-bred animals imported from abroad, and their pure-bred progeny. That first importation in 1916 is so important historically that it is worth recording the details. One of the two stallions was Misanthrope, an iron grey four-year-old who went to Mr Overman's stud, grew to weigh 21 cwt and became one of the finest specimens of the breed in any country. The other, Nonius, was also a grey, he went to the Earl of Lonsdale's stud at Barley Thorpe, Oakham. Nonius was foaled in 1913 and did well, though never quite attaining Misanthrope's size. Lord Lonsdale's six mares were:

Name	Year of birth	Colour	Weight on arrival (lb)
Nicoline	1913	Grey	2,016
Kalidaca	1910	Grey	1,708
Mesniere	1912	White	2,016
Limoselle	1911	Grey	1,708
Nive	1913	Dark Grey	1,708
Neva	1913	Black	1,568

Mr Overman's consisted of:

Name	Year of birth	Colour	Weight on arrival (lb)
Irene	1910	Grey	1,913
Navrante	1913	Black — star	1,652
Ninette	1913	Grey	1,904
Niobe	1913	Grey — star	1,540
Neva	1913	Grey — star	1,792
Nodale	1913	Grey — narrow blaze	1,792

EARLY HISTORY IN FRANCE

Le Perche, south-east of Paris, is the cradle of the Percheron race, and one of the smallest provinces of Old France. The name Perche is said to have come from 'Perticus Saltus', a forest which once covered most of the district. In the ninth century the monks directed considerable clearances, but left many splendid groups of forest trees.

Part of the area is composed of alternate clay, sand and lime, forming moist and fertile soils. Further north, the lime tends to replace the sand which, said the French authority on horse breeding, M Tonnac, is the reason why the more active horses are found in Upper Perche, while the farther south one goes, on to the alluvial soils, the Percherons raised are larger and heavier. The province is suited to grass growing, with temperate climate, annual average rainfall of 35 in, and 100 wet days a year.

Volume 1 of the British Percheron Horse Stud Book, 1922, quotes a fascinating account of French farming in the area. Breeder M Edmond Perriot describes Le Perche farms, which are generally 110 acres in size. The rotation was 22 acres each of winter corn; roots and fallow; spring corn; rotation grasses, and finally 22 acres of permanent pasture. Cultivations were done by four home-reared mares, put to the stallion (either national, approved or authorised) every year. Any not in foal went immediately to town work, being replaced by a two-year-old or three-year-old home-reared filly. The mares earned their keep, and their offspring brought in a yearly net profit to the breeder.

An interesting point about stallion rearing is that 22 acres must not graze more than three two-year-old colts, which are very particular about the choice of grass. Several large stallion establishments in Le Perche had over 1,000 acres of grass.

The history of the Percheron breed resembles that of the Shire on several counts. The Middle Ages were characterised by the powerful charger, barbed with iron and carrying a heavy rider covered in armour. Then in the period following the invention of fire-arms, artillery demanded energetic draught horses and cavalry needed swifter ones. More horses were used on farms. From 1800 to 1860, teams for stage coaches were sought as the road system became established. Then in the post-1860 railway era, the stage coach left the roads and the Percheron became exclusively a heavy draught horse.

While the Percheron charger was reproduced in old illustrations as white or grey, positive information is scarce. A number of Eastern horses probably remained in the country after the disaster that befell the Saracens in 732 between Tours and Poitiers, and if so the energy, strength and distinction suggested by the charger could be attributed to Arab blood.

Early writers claim that a distinction must be made between the Percheron's dappled grey and the grey of the Arab. General Stud Inspector M Quinchez, the then best judge of Arab horses in France, declared: 'The dappled grey of the Percheron is not the grey of the Oriental horses. These are usually pale grey with a few light brown spots; dark spots are very rare. Grey is far from usual in the desert; the chestnut generally predominates among thoroughbreds. I have never seen a dappled grey Arab.'

The grey Percheron coat was in demand in the stage coach era. It made the horses easier to see in the dark, and so preferable for night stages. In the later 19th century American importers favoured a big horse and a black coat. This led to some crossing with Poitou and Nivernais stallions, but such happenings were short-lived, confined to certain stables, and a failure. Then the tide turned, the Americans favoured grey and one great American breeder said: 'Your breed is grey, and if you change the coat you will spoil the breed'.

Between 1820 and 1833 a French stud service was organised for Percherons. Of 43 stallions recorded as having been approved, 38 or 39 were greys. Their lowest height was 15.2 hands with most of them 16 hands and a few 17 hands. There were then some bay mares and a few chestnuts. Thus there was systematic breeding of the heavy draught horse across the Channel well before organised Shire breeding was established in Britain.

By 1900 40 entries were approved at the Pin stallion depot. Of these 22 were grey and 18 black, average height 16 hands, and ranging from 15.3 to 16.2. In 1914, 84 were approved, greys numbered 52 and blacks 32, and the tallest of both measured 17 hands. The 1919 figures show a slight decrease in height, but were taken before the Armistice in November 1918 and were not regarded seriously. The Percheron Horse Society (of France) instituted its stud book in 1883, immediately after the Society was founded. Membership at the end of World War 1 was 2,600.

Of all our modern draught breeds, the Percheron can best claim the trot as a natural gait. To see a pair or a unicorn of grey Percherons gliding into the ring,

Percherons belonging to Vaux Brewery in harness (Gavin Cole).

fore feet reaching out, ears pricked, waggon wheels rumbling, is to be privileged by one of the heavy horse world's finest sights. Yet it has lagged behind other breeds in harness classes and the reasons are difficult to discern. Major A. R. A. Wilson, who managed Vaux Brewery stables at Sunderland, is emphatic that the Percheron has no superior in city traffic and on hard roads.

Its foot gives every appearance of soundness. The hard blue hoof beloved of horsemen is widely found. That part of its ancestry which belonged to the stage coach era no doubt adds the lively turn of speed and it is doubtful if there is now any prejudice because the breed sprang up across the Channel. If recent cattle imports by British livestock men are any indication, jingoistic attitudes among home breeders vanished long ago. The source of so much fresh blood so near is a boon.

BRITISH ORGANISATION

The modern Percheron remains centred in the Eastern Counties, with its headquarters at Cambridge. An annual Show is held each May at Cambridge and is always a thoroughly enjoyable occasion.

If any new starter in the heavy horse world seeks information, they might well consider the Suffolk or Percheron. Clydesdales would probably be the choice in Scotland and possibly in northern England, while Wales is a Shire stronghold, but elsewhere there is much to be said for the clean-legged breeds. The Shire has a highly organised breed secretariat backed by a large and thriving membership. Prices for the best are high. Competition varies from keen to very intense. Because of the sheer number of Shire breeders, it takes time to know and be

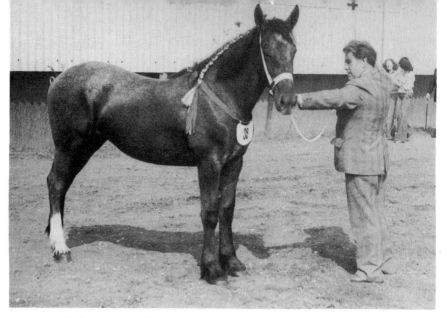

Mr Fred Harlock's young Percheron filly (Audrey Hart).

known. In the Percheron and Suffolk worlds, numbers are at present lower. All newcomers are immediately welcomed, and soon feel one of the band. The atmosphere is generally freer and more relaxed, and a high class Percheron costs considerably less than a Shire of equal show potential. This is not to denigrate the Shire or its organisation in any way; it is simply a question of numbers. Though everyone is made welcome in the Shire world, the newcomer will find his or her feet rather more readily in the numerically smaller breeds.

The newcomer to heavy horses has seldom worked them regularly or been brought up with them. Over three decades, or one and a half human generations, have passed since heavies were part of everyday life. Thus a placid breed is of great advantage. The Percheron fills the bill, and as oft-quoted proof is the practice of running stallions in the same team as mares. Visitors to the Canadian Winter Fair at Toronto have returned full of praise for the American Percherons. Great, strapping horses, they combine in some wonderful 'sixes', the acme of perfection in the North American draught horse world.

As a sire of heavyweight hunters, eventers or show jumpers, the Percheron is under-valued in Britain. Both its clean legs and its temperament give it a decided advantage. In Canada and the USA, the greys and the blacks were used primarily to up-grade common-bred farm stock in the pioneering days. A point that owners of hunter mares and of the lighter types of Thoroughbred might bear in mind is that the stud fee for a Percheron stallion is very much less than for an Arab or race winner. For those who dislike a chestnut riding horse, the blacks and the greys have obvious charm, and add substance and docility to their offspring.

Of 23 stallions registered with the British Percheron Horse Society in 1979-81, five were French-bred. Though no stallions were imported in 1978, three mares crossed the Channel, followed by one in 1979. The imported stallions Mistero

Percheron mare and foal in a crowded summer scene (Audrey Hart).

and Lucasia John Boy have made their mark. Mistero is grey and John Boy black. One of Mistero's 1981 foals was Lime Lady Diana, reflecting the Royal marriage which took place in that year. John Boy came from Canada and one of his colts was sold back across the Atlantic in 1985.

Two English-bred stallions dominated the late 1970s and early 1980s show scene. Three Holes Samson and Willingham Andrew exchanged championship and reserve placings several times, the former taking top place at the breed show in Cambridge in 1982 as a 12-year-old. Andrew was 1985 breed champion, and 15-year-old Samson was reserve.

A blend of French and British blood came to the fore at the 1982 Royal Show. An example was Hardwick Cavalcade, bred by Carl Boyde and sired by the renowned Pinchbeck Union Crest out of the imported Cavale. Reserve at the Royal Show was Abbeythorne Countess, shown by A.S. Johnson and Son Ltd and bred by Fred Harlock. Countess is by Johnson's stallion Three Holes Samson.

Sneath has long been a famous name in the Percheron world, and the family's latest move to improve the breed was the importation of Nurenberg from France. This lovely dapple-grey stallion stands fully 18 hands high and is a powerful getter of excellent foals.

THE BREED IN THE USA

Like so many ultimately successful human enterprises, the introduction of Percherons to the USA began badly. Edward Harris of Moorsetown, New Jersey, had been so impressed with the French heavy draught horse that he imported four head in 1839. Only one, a mare, survived the journey. Not discouraged, Edward Harris returned to France immediately, and purchased two stallions and two

Left *Vaux Brewery Percherons are a common sight in Sunderland.*

Below *G. E. Sneath's well-known grey Percheron stallion Pinchbeck Samuel by Partridge Samuel out of Pinchbeck Lola 2nd (Colin Fry).*

mares, one of which died. There is no record of one stallion, but the other, Diligence, sired almost 100 foals in New Jersey. The horse lived till almost 20, dying in 1856, the year the Crimean War ended. Three Percherons sired by Diligence are named in the American stud book. They are the stallions Diligence II and Louis Philippe, and a mare named Julie, foaled in 1851.

In that same year came two stallions from France that really made their mark, greys named Louis Napoleon and Normandy. Another, Gray Billy, is reputed to have accompanied these two, but his records have been lost. Normandy became know as 'Old Pleasant Valley Bill', and was said to have left an average of 60 foals a year for 18 years. As three-year-olds and four-year-olds these foals sold for $200 apiece, at a time when the country's common stock brought $50 to $125.

Louis Napoleon cost $350 in France. He was chunky, short-legged, and despised by neighbouring horsemen in Ohio. Three years later, when his colts matured, he was acclaimed! This is the over-riding characteristic of the Percherons in their early history in the USA; they proved surprisingly superlative as crossing sires on the general run of farm horses.

While British Shires were being bred on well-established farms and often on prosperous estates owned by the nobility, American farmers were still pioneers, concentrating on working their ever-extending acreages with whatever power they could muster. They were not too concerned about pedigree breeding. The Percherons, and especially Louis Napoleon, proved outstanding for breeding the 'big teams'.

Having changed hands for $1,500, Louis Napoleon became the property of the Dillons of Tazewell County, Illinois, in 1858. The next season he covered only seven mares, but in 1860 the old horse was ridden home during the night to find 42 mares awaiting him. During his time in Illinois he left an estimated 400 foals. He died in 1871, aged 23. His grade colts were sold to farmers at $800 to $1,000 and more — there were no pure-bred Percheron mares in the state at that time. These two stallions, Louis Napoleon and Normandy, impressed fine action and draught qualities on their offspring, and their sons did the same. Yet from 1839 to 1870, only 90 Percheron stallions were imported into the USA, and a mere 20 mares.

The decade following 1870 was one of financial depression. Only 104 stallions and 115 mares were entered in the American Percheron Stud Book in that period. But from 1880, development really took off. From then till 1890, 1,920 Percheron stallions and 2,089 Percheron mares were bred in the USA, and almost 5,000 stallions and 2,566 mares imported.

The century's final decade brought hard times, with a panic collapse of industrial confidence in 1893. Percheron breeders suffered with the rest; good work horses could be bought for $50 or $60 apiece and top-class breeding stock for $100. Horses simply had to be sold to keep families and businesses afloat, and this resulted in sound stock being offered to all and sundry. The Percheron breed thus became more widespread, but benefits were lost when excellent mares went into districts lacking good stallions, or to breeders lacking skill and ambition.

The Boer War (1899-1903) boosted horse exports and the new century's first decade brought growing confidence to farming and in draught horse breeding.

Above *Percherons hauling a self-binder. In most conditions, three or four horses are needed* (Jerry R. Springer).

Below *A magnificent pair of modern American Percherons* (Percheron Horse Association of America).

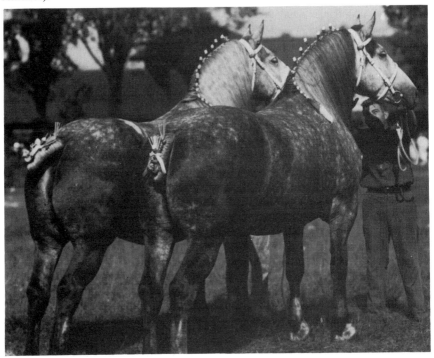

Then came World War 1 and its huge demand for horses. At its close, membership of the Percheron Society of America totalled 11,000, twice the pre-war number. But another slump and the internal combustion engine were at hand.

The American Breed Secretary was then Ellis MacFarland, lucid in his praises:

The big blacks and greys have stood the heat and the cold, the mud and the dust. The mares have been unusually prolific, many producing ten foals and some more. The stallions have such splendid dispositions that many are regularly in the teams with other horses, thereby earning their yearly keep by their work in the collar. Stud fees from such horses have been almost clear profit. It is no uncommon thing to find a Percheron stallion living until he is 20 years old. Mares frequently live until they are 25.

His clean legs, free from hair, enable him to work in mud if necessary and still not be bothered with greasy heel. It takes little work to keep his legs clean. The hard, shiny hoof of the Percheron, with some depth at the heel, stands the wear of our country second to none. His deep middle makes him an easy keeper. Because of his heavy muscling, good action, clean legs, and admirable disposition, he has rightly earned the undisputed title of America's favourite drafter.

With the years the breed has been changed to suit the American breeder. It became the most popular draught breed in the USA, but although it has since lost that position to the Belgian it is still much sought after. The Percheron Horse Association of America boasts 1,000 members, and in 1982 registered 1,251 horses. Probably some 500 breeders are not Association members. At a recent sale in Columbus, Ohio, 100 registered Percherons were entered for the Eastern States Draft Horse Sale. While prices ranged from $2,500 to $7,500 for mares, many topped $5,000. Fillies ranged from $1,000 to $3,700, and aged stallions to $3,700. Starting at $300, the top colts realised $2,100.

IN CANADA

The first record of French horses in Canada dates back to Louis XIV. He sent 20 mares and two stallions from the Royal Stables in 1665, followed by other shipments. These horses remained the King's property for three years, when they were distributed among the gentlemen of the country who had done most to promote colonisation and cultivation.

Few more suitable rewards could be envisaged than these horses who on their home ground became ancestor to the Percheron. Demand for the Canadian animals ebbed and flowed; during foreign wars stock commanded a premium, while in the ensuing slumps they were so very cheap as to be more a liability than an asset. The opening up of the West provided the most consistent market, but the only authentic record of the breed's progress comes from the Canadian Percheron Horse Breeders' Association, initiated in 1907.

Percheron importations and registrations reached their peak from 1917 to 1919, with almost 2,200 imported and over 4,000 registered in the the three years. In the same period well over 3,000 Clydesdales a year were being registered, but their importations had dropped from 1,367 in 1911 to 42 in 1919.

Percheron foals are always born black, though adult colour may be almost white (Audrey Hart).

Rules governing the Association's formation proved so sound that few changes have been needed. Only animals pure-bred on both sides were accepted.

The Percheron's docility was a strong point in its favour. In the 50 years before 1914, skilled, cheap and plentiful horsemen were found in all British farming districts. In Canada that was not so. Teams, and big ones at that, had to be driven by whoever chanced along. A sensible animal was an obvious advantage.

CHARACTERISTICS OF THE PERCHERON

General The British Percheron horse is essentially a heavy draught horse possessing great muscular development combined with style and activity. It should possess ample bone of good quality, and give a general impression of balance and power.

Colour Grey or black, with a minimum of white. No other colour in stallions is eligible for entry in the stud book. Skin and coat should be of fine quality.

Size and weight Stallions should not be less than 16 hands 3 in in height and mares not less than 16 hands 1 in but width and depth must not be sacrificed to height at maturity. Weight of stallions — 18 to 20 cwt; weight of mares — 16 to 18 cwt.

Head Wide across the eyes, which should be full and docile; ears medium in size and erect; deep cheek, curved on lower side, not long from eye to nose; intelligent expression.

Body Strong neck, not short, full arched crest in case of stallions; wide chest, deep well-laid shoulders; back strong and short; ribs wide and deep, deep at flank; hind quarters of exceptional width and long from hips to tail, avoiding any suggestion of a goose rump.

Limbs Strong arms and full second thighs, big knees and broad hocks; heavy flat bone, short canons, pasterns of medium length, feet of reasonable size, of good quality hard blue horn. Limbs as clean and free from hair as possible.

Action Typical of the breed; straight, bold, with a long free stride rather than short snappy action. Hocks well flexed and kept close.

Temperament One of the most docile and good natured of any breed, yet in no way showing any sign of sluggishness or dullness. In stables, or out in the dense town traffic, nothing appears to upset them. This temperament is almost a hundred per cent guarantee of the breed, which makes it possible to switch them from the environment of the farm to that of the busy town with the minimum risk or delay, an often troublesome period with many other breeds.

Stable Management Owing to the almost complete lack of feather and the type of skin, the Percheron can be adequately cared for by the less experienced men we must accept today, with much less risk of galls, itchy legs or poor coats, than would be the case with many other breeds. Their docile nature makes them extremely good to handle.

Working Ability The hoof of the Percheron is of good hard blue horn and very little foot trouble is experienced. The legs too have plenty of good quality bone and despite the body weight usually maintained, stand up very well indeed to the hard roads and permanently studded shoes. As a worker they are willing and genuine almost without exception, and capable of working good loads continuously without undue strain. A pair will take up to $2^1/_2$ tons net load (almost 4 tons gross) on the old type dray with iron tyres, or even a little more on the modern rubber tyred type, averaging two loads a day up to five miles radius and still maintain good condition. The ability to do this work and maintain condition is, it is thought, due to two inherent factors; firstly a very strong consitution and secondly their temperament, which denotes an almost complete lack of nervous tension.

Chapter 8
European and American breeds

Over much of Europe a large number of heavy horse breeds developed, sometimes systematically bred, more often spasmodically. They have often been crossed as occasion demanded, using bigger stallions and stalwart native ponies, much as the Scots developed the Clydesdale from the sound and hardy working horses of the glens and lowlands.

Most of these European breeds were bred, reared and worked on family farms, sometimes under peasant conditions. They have the common quality of docility. With so much family labour employed, starting very young, the farmers and their wives would not countenance vicious animals, just as the Scottish Highlanders kept quiet bulls on their summer shielings or mountain grazings. Toddlers accompanied the herding families, so risks with temperament were not taken. Highland cattle are still quiet today.

Another feature common to the great majority of breeds is that they were affected by mechanisation rather later than were British farm horses. It may well be that revival will start later also. During a visit to Upper Austria in 1982 I had difficulty in finding any interest in draught horses, yet riding was booming there as it was in Britain in the 1970s.

Russia has a number of draught breeds, as may be expected from its vast area. Among them is the Russian Heavy Draught, smaller than most at 14.2 hands. Originating in the Ukraine it is generally chestnut, roan or bay. It has much mane but little feather. In origin it stems back to Swedish Ardennes, Percheron and Orlov Trotter stallions mated to indigenous Ukrainian cart mares in the mid-19th century. The Vladimir Draught stands about 16 hands high and is of any solid colour. Its history dates to 1886 and the use of Clydesdale blood, with a blend of Suffolk, Danish and Dutch.

Another breed based on Russian indigenous types is the Bityug from Voronezh in Russia. It originated from the use of heavy trotting stallions on local mares in the 19th century. It is similar to the Voronezh Coach, the result earlier this century of using Clydesdales on the heavy trotters. From the Baltic shores comes the Lithuanian Heavy Draught, usually chestnut with flaxen mane and tail, but also black, bay, roan or grey. It has dense bone and very little feather. It began from 1879 onwards, when Arab, Ardennes, Shire and Brabancon blood was used on the local Zemaitukai. After 1923-25, Swedish Ardennes stallions were put on

Top *Gavin Cole's Ardennes mare followed by stallion in tandem hitch (Gavin Cole).*

Above *Ardennes mare (Cogvette) with a week old foal. Bred by Gavin Cole in County Durham (Gavin Cole).*

Below *How the French show teams of horses. Family group at the Ardennes National championships, Vittel, France 1981 (Gavin Cole).*

Ardennes stallion in the show ring, Ardennes National Championship, Vittel, France, 1981
(Gavin Cole).

the type which was recognised as a separate breed in 1963.

The Murakoz from Hungary suffered during World War 2, having been a prime source of farm power between the Wars. It is usually chestnut, often with flaxen mane and tail, but other whole colours occur. Slightly lighter is the Yugoslav Draught, usually chestnut or brown, with both Ardennes and Pinzgau blood in it. The Pinzgau is a mountain breed, more sure-footed than most heavies, and some horses have the eye-catching tiger spots. It is of Austrian derivation.

The Italian Heavy Draught comes from the northern and central areas of that country, and is a dark liver chestnut with chestnut or blond mane and tail. It is now bred more for meat than work.

If the Italian Heavy Draught has an unusual colour, the Poitevin or Poitou has a special purpose. Originally imported from the North European flatlands, it was used to drain the region's marshes, helped by its enormous feet. That task accomplished, it might well have slipped into obscurity and extinction but for its great value as the dam of large and valuable mules. Its stud book started in 1885, and it has been termed the Poitevin mulassier (mule producer). Jacks of the tall baudet Poitevin strain are used to produce big black or dark brown mules, full of hair.

The Ardennes is now well known in Britain. It is comparatively short and very thick set, with a massive forehand, chest and forearms. It is claimed to be more easily kept than the taller Shire and better able to subsist on hill grazings. Certainly it is by no means as flashy as the Shire or Clydesdale, and is very much a utilitarian

The two-year-old UK bred Ardennes mare Morag. The first to be born in the North of England for over 50 years (Gavin Cole).

animal. British breeders have imported the Ardennes, which has a determined, if placid nature. A product of north-east France, its stud book was formed in 1908-14 and again in 1923. It is usually a shade of roan, bay or chestnut. Its breeding is a matter of detailed concern and a class of Ardennes at regional shows is an impressive sight. Protagonists claim that its short legs and immense strength make it a far better farmer's horse than Britain's native breeds, but others do not care for its unresponsive nature.

The Dutch Draught Horse is the Netherlands' most numerous heavy. Short-necked with a comparatively small head, it has a massive and deep body of bay, chestnut or grey colour. Leg feather is darker. It is similar to the Belgian, due to Belgian blood from circa 1889 onwards. The stud book was opened in 1915.

The Rhenish comes from the Rhine Valley and is another breed derived from the Belgian. Its stud book was founded in 1876, and there are a number of regional offshoots. It stands 16 to 16.2 hands and is clean-legged. The Rhenish was used to found the Black Forest which is chestnut with light mane. The parent breed is sorrel, roan or brown, with the light mane and tail.

An eastern Normandy breed seen by Ralph Whitlock is the Augeron, which he described as very similar to the Boulonnais. Mason in *A Dictionary of Livestock Breeds* points to some Norman and Percheron blood, and as the Boulonnais resembles the Percheron, both authorities are right. Though usually grey or black like the Percheron, the Boulonnais may also be red roan, blue roan or bay. It shows traces of Arab blood in its slightly concave face, and stands 16 to 17 hands.

From Denmark comes the Jutland, usually chestnut, which was improved by the importation of a Shire stallion in 1862. Its breed society was formed in 1888. East Anglian enthusiasts doubtless claim that the Schleswig is a further improvement, for it springs from the use of a Suffolk stallion on Jutland mares!

The Finnish Draught is another north European breed that was derived from large stallions from western Europe on indigenous forest mares. It was usually chestnut, sometimes brown, and became an all-round farm horse. Judging by performance rather than breed type or pedigree is common and, as is usual in areas of family farms, the Finnish has a generally sweet disposition.

BRABANCON

One of the largest and heaviest of the European breeds is the Brabancon or Brabant from Belgium. The term is less used now than Belgian, which formed its own breed society in 1886, and its stud book in 1890. It was known in France as the cheval de gros trait Belge (Belgian heavy draught horse). In Volume I of that stud book of the Société Nationale des Eleveurs Belges, secretary Chevalier Hynderick wrote:

> The races of Belgian horses of trade generally grouped into three great classes; first the Flemish horse in the North West part of Western Flanders; second the Ardenne of Luxembourg and Namur; and third the Brabancon horse brought up in the rest of the country. Two pure races will always be found in Belgium, and one of these the Ardenne originated in the valley of the Meuse; the other Frisonne race of which one variety, the Flemish, is found on the border of the sea. It is from the union of these two races that we get the Brabancon horse.

The first Belgian Stud Book in its native country was dated 1878. At the 1880 National Show in Brussels, where the best horses were presented, entries totalled 625. They comprised 276 bays, 81 chestnuts, 41 blacks, 93 greys, 15 black-

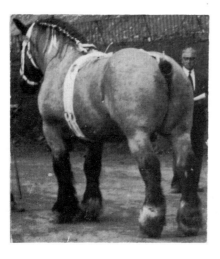

Left *Quo Vadis Des Volees, a native Belgian bay roan stallion of the 1950s* (Rottiers).

Right *Belgian horses at work in Belgium* (Rottiers).

roans, 82 bay-roans and 34 chestnut-roans. Numbers had risen to 740 for the 1904 National Show. They included 323 bays, 262 chestnuts, 25 blacks, 22 greys, 15 black-roans, 65 bay-roans and 28 chestnut-roans.

From being a sizeable minority, the bay-roans rose from 13.12 per cent in 1880, and 8.78 per cent in 1904 to 30 per cent in 1932. At the National Show in that year, entries totalled 755, with 230 bays, 227 bay-roans, 216 chestnuts, 61 chestnut-roans, 17 black-roans, two blacks, two greys. By 1939 the greys had disappeared at the National event and, in this final display before World War 2 swept away so much of Belgian life and tradition, the 684 entries comprised 231 bay-roans (33.78 per cent), 194 chestnuts, 196 bays, 53 chestnut-roans, six blacks and four black-roans.

In 1978, 169 stallions were authorised in Belgium among the Belgian and Ardennes breeds, the latter in that country being a smaller Belgian. There were 102 bay-roans, including three very dark ones. The 53 bays included four dark and four very light, while the six chestnut-roans included two very dark. Of the seven black-roans, four were the usual shade and three very light, and only one black.

The colour description, kindly sent to me by M Laurent Rottiers, needs amplification. He says: 'In Belgium, the Netherlands, Germany and France, one never speaks of a brown horse. What Anglo-Saxon horsemen and breeders call a *brown* is always mentioned as *bay* or *dark bay*.

'Even if the French or Germans speak of a 'bai-brun' or a 'schwarzbraun', they never consider it an independent colour, but always as a darker bay than the common ones. Because of this, some inexperienced Continentals thought, by reading British or American books, that *brown* meant the darkest shade (almost my favourite colour) or liver chestnut.'

There is scope for confusion here, for in the United Kingdom a bay by definition is a shade of brown with black points, ie, black mane, tail and feet. If its mane and tail are not black, but follow its body colour, then it is a brown or a

A grand type of American Belgian.

chestnut. A bay may have a darker body colour than a brown, provided its points
fit the definition.

AMERICAN BELGIAN

Many wealthy American owners took up Belgian breeding after 1918, and tended
to dominate the show rings. They bred for a more upstanding horse, one with lots
of flash and action, and more suitable for commerical hitches than for farming.
The spread of the American Belgian is one of the post-World War 2 phenomena.
There is nothing in the heavy horse world to approach it, and the type evolved in
North America is so far distant from European Belgians that breeders crossing the
Atlantic had difficulty in accepting that the two were once the same stock.

The Brabant was the founder of the American Belgian or 'race de trait Belge'.
American importers preferred firstly sorrel, then strawberry roan. This suited
everyone, as the Belgian breeders of last century did not like sorrels, and were glad
to part with them to American buyers. In fact they were not prepared to part with
much else, and this accounts for the sorrel colouring of the American Belgian
breed, and answers the question as to where the American colour came from. The
stallion Orange I is regarded as the pillar of the Brabant breed, and was founder of

the 'gros de la Bendre' line of massive, heavy, deep bay horses. Another group or line of breeding was founded by the stallion Bayard or 'gris du Hainaut', with colour of dun, sorrel and grey. A third group or line was founded by a bay horse, Jean I.

In 1878 Brilliant, the son of Orange I, won the International championship in Paris and in the succeeding years won at London, Lille and Hanover. These achievements brought the Belgian breed right to the fore, and its position was reinforced when Reve D'Or won the world championship in 1900. Of the modern Brabants, the most famous was Avenir d'Herse.

Roans and bays fell from favour, and it was evident that the top breeders were eliminating them altogether. At the International in Chicago and at the various County and State Fairs the sorrel Belgian with white mane and tail became all the rage; even the chestnuts were being displaced. There was nothing in the standard of points for judging Belgian horses to indicate any discrimination against bays or roans, but it was found that colour did play a big part in the final placings among animals of equal conformation. Soon the breeders realised that if they wanted to take the top prizes, they began with a distinct disadvantage if their horses did not sport the sorrel body colour and accompanying white mane and tail.

If they had the low-down, short-legged, typical Belgian horses of the old

A team of Belgians hauling a gang plough.

country, they were also badly placed for the hitch or harness classes. The showmen wanted a taller horse with more action, the flashy colour of a smart red-sorrel, with white mane, tail and very often some white on the legs. White spots on the body or any quantity of feather were definitely out.

Remember that mechanisation swept North American farming and transport before World War 2, whereas in the United Kingdom the great change came during and after the War. Even in the 1930s, some County and State Fairs in the USA had dropped draught horse classifications, and the breeding and showing of all draught breeds was at a low ebb. Fortunately, though numbers had declined, standards hadn't, and when the USA and world economy strengthened, so did the affairs of the Belgian horse. It was overhauling the Percheron as the most popular breed.

Now the Draught Horse Hitch or Harness classes, or turn-outs in British terminology, have been re-introduced. Show secretaries discovered that the crowds left after the last heavy horse class, even thought the light breeds were still competing. The hitch classes include single cart, pairs, four and, the present highlight of the North American heavy horse show world, sixes. And Belgians predominate in them.

In the horse pull contest a team pulls a weighted sledge, to which more weights are added until only the winners can move the requisite distance. Many more Belgians than any other breed take part.

The Belgian's temperament is generally sound, whether for work, breed classes, in harness, or for a pulling contest. It is backed by an active and energetic breed society, the Belgian Draft Horse Corporation of America, which continues to boost the interests of the entire heavy horse world.

That the Belgian is still booming is shown by latest figures from the Belgian

Top right *An American Belgian braided for showing. Note the style compared with British dressing.*

Left *Award-winning American Belgians.*

Draft Horse Corporation of America. Membership in 1983 rose to 3,500, and 1,500 registrations were completed in 1982. There were 5,677 transfers completed for breeders in 44 States and five Canadian Provinces. At the Ohio sales in February 1983, Belgian stallions sold for up to $10,750, averaging $1,650, while mares averaged $2,678 to a top of $9,100. Geldings averaged $1,729, peaking at $4,650. At the Indiana sale in March 1983, 150 head of heavy horses were sold. There the top gelding made $4,400, with mares to $7,350 and stallions to $7,750.

Secretary Francis Eustis, of 8450 Eustis Farm Lane, Cincinnati, Ohio 45243, sums up: 'The colour of the "American Belgian" is sorrel (blonde to dark chestnut), white manes and tails preferred; white on legs and a stripe on the face; no spots on body. Roan and bay have been pretty well eliminated through selection. This I personally feel is wrong, because colour should not predominate over type and conformation. If you could be at one of our big shows you would like them; the best of disposition, and overall a damn good horse in scale, type and conformation.'

Chapter 9
North America and the big teams

When North America was first peopled by Europeans, the early settlers naturally turned to the breeds of horse that they knew at home to provide power to break the prairies and haul fencing material on the range. The settlers bred and sold horses to the road and rail construction companies. Until those railways were connected, waggon trains were the main form of overland transport, and a ten-by-ten outfit consisted of ten waggons with ten span of oxen for each. Oxen were preferrred to horses, for they could live off the natural vegetation as they went along.

The Oregon Trail was a severe test for horses even without work. One batch of 12 Percheron mares and a stallion was reduced to three mares by its journey's end. Other imports came from ships that had sailed round the Horn, a desperate journey for men and horses alike. The Oregon Horse and Land Company imported over 100 Percherons from France.

Even in 1845, the Willamette Valley was reported to have 1,716 heavy horses, of Clydesdale, Percheron and Belgian breeding. The 1869 Oregon Territory census recorded over 50,000 horses, mules and asses. Yet nothing like sufficient horses could be imported to supply the ever-expanding needs of tillage, harvest and transport. Mowing machines and threshers were spreading in the 1850s, and horses stronger than the plentiful Indian ponies were needed.

The wind of change blew yearly on the North American corn lands. Each new development was followed by another which enabled one man to plough and work more and more acres, handle more and more hay and corn. While in Britain one horseman per team of two was standard, and remained so until 1939, in North America teams of six, eight or 16 horses were commonplace, and from 16 to 44 when combine harvesters were introduced.

It was soon found that the pure heavy breeds were not nimble enough for the big teams. If weighing more than about 1,450 lb, the horses were unwieldy en masse; they were cramped if yoked close together, and slow and difficult on hillsides and corners. Nor did the first cross Clydesdale or Percheron stallion on the wiry Indian pony provide a suitable animal. The offspring at 1,000 or 1,100 lb were still too small. But a Thoroughbred x Indian pony put to a Clydesdale entire was just right, throwing a horse of 1,350 lb average.

The breeding techniques in no way followed the precise British method of a registered stallion on his regular round, walked by a professional stud groom. The settlers fenced an area round a water supply in such a fashion that the Thoroughbred stallion could not jump out, but with the bottom rail high enough for the Indian mare to pass under. Three or four years later, the Thoroughbred was replaced by a Clydesdale stallion, the young crossbred mares came in to visit him, and in due time produced white-faced, white-footed foals of just the type for the big teams.

These teams lived chiefly off by-products. 'Wheat hay' was cut when the ear was milky, from the outside of the corn fields, the early operation clearing a track for the binder or combine. In winter the main feed was straw containing a proportion of grain lost through inefficient separating, and as spring approached, the teams were brought into barns and fed a small ration of grain plus hay. In summer they grazed a winter variety of wheat sown in the spring, and producing flag or leaf rather than ears.

A few of the heavier horses made up logging teams, where real weight was required. Most logging teams were of two horses of at least 1,600 lb each. For very big trees, two and two would be harnessed. Commands were commonly by voice alone. A ranch near Hay Station, Washington, had some 200 Percheron mares. Their gelding offspring weighed 1,600 to 1,800 lb as four-year-olds, and were sold in strings, tied literally head to tail, for logging. Horses were used for this work well into the 1930s.

A combine harvester cuts and threshes the standing crop of corn in one operation. It is thus unlike the self binder, which delivers neatly tied sheaves that must then be stooked, led to the stack, thatched, and handled all over again on to the thresher. The first successful grain combine was built in Michigan about 1836, but not till the 1850s did the machines become popular, and large-scale

The big team in action showing one of the early American combine harvesters.

Eight-horse team in American hitch with cultivator, driven by Mark Morton (Gavin Cole).

manufacture spread in the 1880s. These combines required much horse power to operate them. Over 30 horses might be needed to pull the machines and work the cutting and threshing mechanism via the drive wheels.

EQUALISING HITCHES

It is one thing to yoke a team of 16 horses to one implement, and quite another to ensure that each pulls its share. Some horses develop a knack of appearing to pull when all they are doing is keeping their traces taut. Though the big team driver kept a can of stones handy to fling at offenders, equalising the load was not easy without a proper hitch.

Many types were tried, the most popular being the Schandoney Equalizing Hitch, patented in 1893. Peter Schandoney was driving a ten-mule plough team on his family's farm in the Sacramento Valley, using the 'dead hitch' consisting of five pairs in tandem, and he observed that the more energetic mules pulled most of the load, while the lazy ones boxed themselves to avoid much pulling. The 'clover leaf' is the basis of the Schandoney hitch. By its use the driver can readily observe which units of the team are pulling their weight, and act accordingly. Working on the leverage principle, it can be adapted for any number of horses.

It must always be remembered that these 'big team' horses and mules were not broken in the British sense. If they saw the inside of a collar six times they were considered broken. They were not painstakingly 'mouthed' or groomed, or taught to have their feet picked up. They were taught the rudiments and then packed in behind two, three or four fast-walking, strong and intelligent lead horses.

The great lead horses of the New Countries deserve a place in history. Without them, the rest of the available horse power would have been largely wasted. Through their sense and steadiness they enabled a motley gang of horses to be worked by one man. We must recognise the conditions under which they operated. The large tracts of land were often unfenced; the cropped area simply petered out where the hills became too steep or the ground too stony.

'Breakaways' were commonplace, and only the leaders prevented many more.

In a team of 18, comprising three lines of six abreast, the lead horses were a long, long way from the driver. Even on his high perch he had difficulty in seeing the extent of the ground, just where the turn should be made, or when to start turning so that the machine remained in motion. Reliable lead horses helped a difficult task. Another point was that the big team might have to be driven by whoever chanced along. The homesteader made do with what labour he could muster and the wanderers were by no means always skilled horsemen. If they could manage to control the leaders, the work was done somehow.

These horses were usually geldings, powerful and of raking stride, for on their pace depended that of the whole team. They had to be strong, for on their efforts depended the direction taken by the seething mass of horseflesh behind them.

DRIVING

The horse's herd instinct plays a large part in big team operation. Standard equipment helps. Yoking 32 animals to a combine could take half the morning if slick routine was not devised and followed.

While British horsemen usually used knots for fastening and unfastening their reins, and could tie them safely and speedily, tying and untying 32 horses was a very different matter. Snap lines were universal among the big teams, and a system of 'tying in and bucking back' was devised to give control over every animal. Only the outside lead horses had reins attached. In some cases a single line, the 'jerk-line', controlled the whole team. Other horses in the lead team were controlled by check straps and jockey sticks, which in effect were light sticks strong enough to keep the horses apart, whereas chains or ropes prevented them moving too far sideways.

To turn left using the jerk-line, the driver exerted a steady pull which caused the jerk-line horse to move sideways to the left, and the rest of the team had little option but to follow. When moving to the right, the driver gave a series of short jerks, which made the horse lift its head and step sideways to the right, followed by the rest. After a time each horse understood its duties, and jockey sticks and check straps could be dispensed with.

An example of the big teams used to haul waggons over rough country (Kendall Webb).

Two lines were used on steep slopes, and occasionally four. In the latter case, there were two for the lead team and two for the six animals immediately behind them. These six could then begin their turn before the lead team and reduce the load on them. In a 33-horse combine team, the three lead horses did not pull the machine. Their strength was used to lead and guide the other 30, which were divided into five teams of six abreast. In a 44-horse team there were four leaders and five teams of eight abreast.

American agricultural and engineering colleges played an important part in developing big team techniques. The Horse and Mule Association of America tested their findings and helped spread the gospel in the fields. Precise measurements were necessary, as an inch on the evener swingle tree could create side draught or cause chafing to some unfortunate horse because a chain was not in quite the right position. Three fundamentals were borne in mind. Side draught of the implement must be reduced to the minimum or eliminated; the load must be equalised so that no animal could idle; and each must have as much room and comfort as possible.

Drivers thought in terms of teams rather than individuals. The horses were taken from the stable or barn to their work as a team; they were watered in fours, fives or sixes or however many were working abreast. They returned to the implement as a team, swinging into regular working positions as they stopped. Long feed and water troughs facilitated these manoeuvres.

OUTPUT

While one acre per day was standard for a two-horse team, a 16-horse team pulling four furrows could turn over 18 acres a day of level land. An eight-foot seed drill pulled by four horses would sow 18 to 20 acres daily, while six horses and a ten-foot drill accomplished 25 acres. A six-horse team yoked to a 24-foot drag harrow could cover 35 acres a day. One man and eight horses sufficed for 320 acres of corn land, while three men could manage 1,000 acres. Such figures approximate to British output on arable farms of the 1980s, but the yields today are so many times higher per acre that any comparison is misleading.

Horse power was also used for tasks done later by stationary engines, to power threshing machines, and derricks to lift sacks. The horses walked round and round the 'merry-go-round' at speeds of just over two miles per hour, their forward movement being converted into rotary power by a series of cogs and shafts.

Chapter 10
Carts and waggons

There is a certain cult worship of those former generations of wheelwrights whose enduring workmanship so delights us today. The men themselves would have scoffed. They did not regard themselves even as craftsmen; they were simply ordinary village folk doing a job by very well defined rules.

Some envy the simplicity of those Victorian and Edwardian days, but they were sheer hard work. Hours were long, wages low, and for the employers there was the constant worry of agricultural depression which cut down their trade and made payments tardy and uncertain. A joiner from the 1920s told me how they had to trudge knee-deep in sawdust and shavings for days on end. Consideration of working conditions was low on the agenda, or absent altogether. To make the lot of the apprentice easier was 'encouraging idleness', a deadly sin of that era.

There was nothing leisurely about the work. Everything was made from the raw materials on hand. I still have a screw driver and mallet made by my grandfather, a village joiner and wheelwright up to the end of World War 1. A barrow wheel

A farm tip-cart with horse dressed out for showing.

A pair of bay/roan Shire geldings pulling a modern rubber-tyred waggon at the 1980 South of England Show. Owned and driven by Mr Frank Thomas, Kent. (Colin Fry).

had to be made in a day, starting from the three different types of wood in blocks for naff, spokes and felloes. Much of the timber was locally grown, and selected by the wheelwright as it grew. It was felled and left to season, being cut into lengths over a saw pit by hand. The man below was showered in sawdust throughout the operation.

Oak, ash and elm were the main timbers. Elm was used for the nave, hub, naff, or central part of the wheel. It did not split, and so was also a favourite for chair seats. The spokes radiating from it were of seasoned oak. They were shaped by hand to fit exactly into the nave at one end and into the ash felloes at the other. Each felloe normally took two spokes, so wheels always have an even number of spokes. These felloes formed the circumference and when the wheel was assembled it was bound by an iron tyre.

The hot iron was cooled and so shrank on to the wheel, remaining tight. This tyring process was carried out at the blacksmith's which, in my grandfather's case and many others, was adjacent to the wheelwright's. The tyre was placed on an open fire of peat, straw or shavings, with the untyred wheel placed on a heavy tyring platform, with a central hole to take the hub. Spokes and felloes were supported by the platform for their entire length.

Two or three men grasped the now hot tyre with long-handled tyring tongs, threw it on to the ground to dislodge fuel and foreign matters, then lifted it again and lowered it into position around the wheel. Levers termed tyre dogs were used in combination with a heavy hammer to bring the tyre exactly into position. Cold water was then poured on to the rim which contracted and shrank. Needless to say, considerable experience was needed to make the whole operation a lasting success.

BUILDING A WAGGON

Though waggon building is a traditional skill, it is very much part of the present. Coach builders like Joe Thompson, Thinford House, Thinford, Spennymoor, on the very edge of industrial Durham, are still building to well-tried specifications. They incorporate modern materials where practical.

'I start with the axles, and build up from there', said Joe Thompson. 'The wheels are purchased separately, and we would make our own only if we had the right equipment. Otherwise the process is too slow for today's needs.'

The wheels he buys for a new dray have bevelled edges. The iron rim is wider than the felloes, and this projection cushions the wheel if it scrapes a kerb-stone. If the tyre was flush with the felloes, the spokes would be liable to scratching by any obstructions. The springs are bought from a specialist spring maker, and their fitting is vital. The height of the wheels plus springs governs the future balance and appearance.

Right *Brake block on brewer's show dray.*

Below *Axle-arm, farm waggon.*

A body of ash cross-members houses the lock or turntable — the 'fifth wheel', as American horsemen term it. The facing iron rings are so housed to enable the vehicle to turn at a sharp angle. Oak and ash are used for the body frame, and the floor is of one inch ash or elm. Sides are of mahogany, the only timber readily available in sufficient width, for each side is made of a single piece. 'Though expensive, it is possible to buy mahogany of exactly the right width, 20 inches in this case', explained Joe Thompson, handling the green-painted dray he made for Mr Henry of Ponteland, Northumberland. 'If the piece is too long, we can use the extra to make a side for a smaller vehicle of some sort.'

Though it seems almost a shame to paint such lovely wood, a bright colour is needed, and varnish does not last long enough. A diamond tread plate for safety is fitted under the coachman's feet, and his seat fits into strong iron slots. The name plate is similarly fitted behind the coachman, being arched above his head. A traditional foot brake is cable-operated, the pedal being a vital feature as the coachman may well have his hands literally full if he has four horses in front of him.

Selection of material is as vital to the modern coach maker as ever it was. Though it is seldom possible to buy a standing tree, fell it and air-dry it, only the best timber is bought. Joe Thompson has a whole stack of elm logs drying, destined for future hubs as the horse-drawn wheels of Britain become widespread once again.

HISTORY OF THE CART AND WAGGON

The cart is a two-wheeled vehicle, the waggon has four wheels. The standard for a farm cart in an arable district is a capacity for one ton, drawn by one horse, with trace horse in front if the slope demands it. A single axle takes the cart's two wheels and the weight of the body. Cart remains have been discovered in the fourth-century BC village of Glastonbury.

The cart's load must be balanced evenly, otherwise it becomes 'light on' if weighted towards the rear, and the shafts ride upwards, putting the horse at a disadvantage. Too much weight in front makes the cart 'heavy on', entailing needless pressure on the horse's back. The careful horseman puts his crooked arm under the shaft end from time to time; if he can lift it fairly easily, the load is balanced, but if he cannot there is too much weight forward, and adjustments must be made.

No such balancing act is needed in the waggon, but it takes a bigger draught than the cart, and is not as handy for reversing in a confined space. To haul a waggon over a sound road surface requires one third more power from the horse compared with hauling a cart. On the softer conditions of arable land, still bigger differences are registered.

Far left *Underside of fore-carriage on a traditional farm waggon.*

Left *Dish of waggon-wheel.*

Right *A new use for an old cart.*

Above *Horses drawing a Wolds waggon in the Walkington Hayride. Note the pole and traces which mark out this type from the more usual shafted waggon. On the steep hillsides of the Wolds, less damage was done if a load tipped over (Gavin Cole).*

Above right *A market van built around 1900 and owned by Mr C. R. Fewster, Harrow Farm, Charlton Village, Shepperton, Middlesex. The Shire gelding Broadley Monarch is driven by Ernie Winslade (Colin Fry).*

Below *A three, a two and a single. The leading team is a 'unicorn', with two wheelers and one leader. This is a difficult hitch to drive as the leader has no companion, and so must be fast walking, responsive and intelligent (Gavin Cole).*

Waggons were mainly confined to the more level parts of England and Wales; Scotland does not possess local types. This is strange, as the best Scottish arable is just as workable as the English lowlands. The Scots went in for speed and action rather than sheer weight, and weight is undoubtedly necessary to move weight in the horse world.

Some contemporary writers on equine matters spell waggon with a single 'g'. Throughout this book the double 'g' is always used for horse-drawn vehicles, the single 'g' being reserved for motorised wagons. It is done on no less an authority than Fowler's classic *Modern English Usage*:

'The Oxford English Dictionary gives precedence to *wagon*, but concludes its note on the two forms with: "In Great Britain *waggon* is still very commonly used; in the U.S. it is rare". Counting its post-18th-c. quotations we find 35 *waggon* to 11 *wagon* and it is clear that *waggon* is the British form.'

The first horse-drawn vehicles were primitive indeed, and in poorer areas improvements were long arriving. Even two centuries ago George Culley could describe how in Scotland he had 'many times seen a horse and cart conveying peats or turves, when the whole apparatus contained neither iron, leather nor hemp. The collar or braham was made of straw, the backband of plaited rushes, and the wheels of wood only, without bush of metal, or binding of iron.'

It seems that waggons first came to Britain from the Netherlands. Dutchmen in the 16th century were engaged in draining the Fens, and brought with them equipment to which they were accustomed.

There are two main types of waggon, the box and the bow. The former is found in Wales, Yorkshire, the Eastern Counties and the south-east. It generally has a deep body, whereas the bow waggon has more elegant curves and lighter timbering. Along the north banks of the Bristol Channel across the south

Top left Mr Ted Dunning of York with a farm rulley that he bought for half a crown in the 1950s.

Above left Kent, hop waggon.

Left Part of the summer scene. A 'line up' of 'turnouts' at a typical country show (Colin Fry).

Top Black Shire gelding driven to a Rutland waggon at the South of England Show, Ardingly, Sussex. Owners are Mr and Mrs Izzard (Colin and Janet Fry).

Above Hermaphrodite, English fens.

Midlands, and roughly south to the Isle of Wight and into the south-west peninsula, the bow waggon holds sway.

WELSH FARM VEHICLES

John Thompson has facilitated the spread of detailed information on historic waggons by supplying a series of plans of various types.

One of the most significant agricultural vehicles preserved in Britain is the Welsh Ewenni Ox-wain. It may be seen at the St. Fagan's Welsh Folk Museum, and is the probable fore-runner of the bow waggon.

The Glamorgan waggon is arguably the most elegant of British types, with an astonishing amount of intricate workmanship. According to C. Fox, writing in *Antiquity*, 1931, 'they possess the seemingly inevitable beauty and fitness of the last days of the sailing ships and other specialised creations which have been perfected by generations of men content to work in one tradition.'   Panelled sides are a feature of the bow waggon, with bowed raves over the rear wheels, and a spindled aperture above each end. The Glamorgan waggon colour is blue, with red under-parts. A semi-circular painted board bearing the name and address of the owner is fixed to the ribs of the front board, usually in black and white.

Blue is also the colour of some Monmouthshire waggons, especially near the borders of Herefordshire, but yellow is the dominant hue. A similar but smaller waggon comes from the Forest of Dean, used by the part-time farmers there who were also miners. Both coal and farm produce were hauled.

The Welsh Cob is an all-purpose animal and was used for farm work in Wales. This stallion was owned by Mr Gerry Sowerby.

Glamorganshire waggon.

The Radnorshire waggon is painted Prussian blue and operated in a more hilly district than most. The waggons were used more for road work, including transport of cider apples, stones, or root crops, and the framework was accordingly strong.

Two other Welsh waggons are the Denbighshire and the Montgomeryshire. The former is also found in Anglesey, and side planks, undercarriage and floor boards are much heavier than on most farm waggons. Stones were often carried in the Montgomeryshire version, which was built accordingly. This waggon was less often used for harvest as its area bordered moorland and was away from the main waggon zones.

The Gambo was simply a frame on wheels and when loaded with hay was mainly invisible under its canopy. The wheels were protected by perpendicular rails or ladders. A restored Gambo is on display at the Welsh Folk Museum.

The Welsh Long Cart fitted the Welsh lanes, it was long and narrow. Similar carts were used in Scotland and the north of England. The latter region has some very large carts rather than a range of waggons found further south. The Northumberland harvest cart has open, spindle sides and nicely curved rails.

WAGGONS ABROAD

In the New Countries, the early settlers seem to have chosen waggons. Man rather than horse was the chief limiting factor, and as a large team could be harnessed to one waggon and still be driven by one person, it was a more economical method of transport.

Rittenhouse lists 48 different types of American waggon, against only four carts. The waggons usually had seats — none of the old-time English foremen being around to scoff — and for the most part were strictly functional, rectangular boxes. They were built to serve an immediate purpose rather than a future generation. Heavy brakes were a feature of the mountain waggons, with body 12 ft long and rear wheels 4 ft 4 in high. The hay waggons, circa 1885, had some of the curves of the traditional British versions, though perhaps derived more directly from the Conestoga waggon.

The Conestoga waggon was first designed in the Conestoga Valley of Lancaster County in 1755. It was constructed specifically for the early trails, and generally hauled by six horses. Its huge wheels and rugged workmanship enabled it to ford streams and cross rough, unroaded country without being shaken apart. The Conestoga's capacity was enormous. It resembled a sea-going boat rather than farm transport and, like the 'prairie Schooner' of Gold Rush days, had a top cover over a hooped framework. An outstanding example is to be found in the American Museum near Bath, dated circa 1830. Another waggon with top bows was the Texas. It had a canvas top, but came on the scene later than the old 'covered waggons'.

In 1893 aluminium was used for the metal parts of the Studebaker waggon, an expensive, lavishly decorated show piece. The box was of rosewood, the border of holly, and three months' work and 30 processes were needed for finishing the rare wood. The 'fifth wheel' design enabled acute turns to be negotiated. The fifth wheel was horizontal, and over the centre of the front axle, giving stability. The weight was spread evenly over this large, flat wheel, whereas with other types of turntable there was more risk of upsetting the whole vehicle. Studebakers also made durable farm waggons (with seats) whose deep body sides were finished in green with red trim and red wheels. The firm is one of many that passed into the automobile world.

For really heavy loads, springless waggons were used, and these were termed 'dead-axle drays' in America. One with high, railed sides could carry four tons, and needed a good horseman in charge of the dray with its 14 ft length and 50 in width. Its wheels were broad-tyred rather than tall, 38 in at the rear and 34 in in front, both extending beyond the body. A Transfer Dray was used for theatrical scenery, newsprint rolls and pipes or poles. The beer waggon was also dead-axle, with simple racks for the kegs, and a large canvas parasol above the the driver's seat.

Chapter 11
Model horse-drawn vehicles

Interest in making miniature vehicles has become so strong that there is now a Model Horse Drawn Vehicles Society. Plans for a wide range of models may be obtained from John Thompson, 1 Fieldway, Calthorpe Park, Fleet, Hampshire. These include the Conestoga waggons with which the early settlers crossed the North American continent.

Modelling is an ideal hobby for those who worked with the carts and waggons in their youth, but it is by no means confined to the older generation. The finished models make ideal gifts and command a useful price, though barely commensurate with the number of hours involved if viewed commercially.

DETAIL

Attention to detail is a top priority with any model horse-drawn vehicles' enthusiast. Each part of the harness has a specific function and if it does not fit properly the horse is uncomfortable. It can then no more work properly than we can if our clothes do not fit, with the added danger of chafing through rubbing at the vital points, under the saddle and the collar.

So a collar that moves all over the place at a touch would be quite unacceptable to those very skilled generations of old-time horsemen, and should be so today when the model maker applies the finishing touches. The saddle girth must be

Whippletree (tubular).

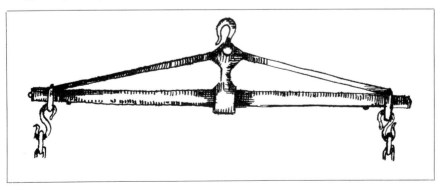

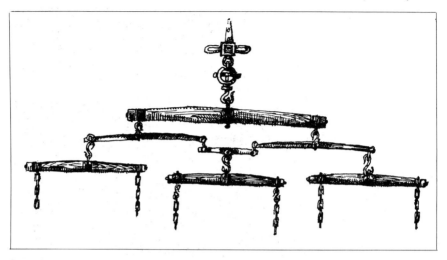

Above *Three-horse swing-trees.*

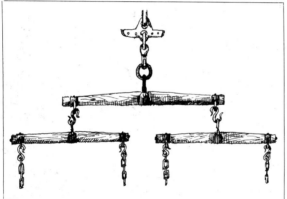

Left *Swing-trees for a heavy pair.*

Right *The Scottish peaked collar is a distinctive feature (Audrey Hart).*

reasonably tight, but the belly band, the strap that joins the shafts underneath the horse, should have a hand's play on the live animal. Its function is to prevent the cart shafts rising in the air if too much weight is put on the back of the cart. When the animal is reversed, the shafts tend to rise and the belly band prevents this happening.

Breechings harness comes into play only when the horse is going downhill or backing its load. At other times it should lie slack, but not too slack, around the haunches. The chains that attach the harness to the shafts are important. The parts fixed to the harness are small and strong, culminating in bigger links to hook over the metalwork of the shafts. These larger links should be of specific number. They form the adjustment that can be varied according to the size of animal. And of course they must be the same length on either side. The old-time foremen would be horrified if a horse was not yoked correctly and precisely, and the model maker must apply the same standards.

The horses themselves are of four main breeds, Clydesdale, Percheron, Shire and Suffolk. Clydesdales are brown, bay or black, often with white legs. Other Clydesdale colours are roan in various shades, from strawberry to blue roan, and occasionally grey. That colour is rare in the breed, and best avoided. A point to remember with Clydesdales is that they may be wearing the attractive Scottish high peak harness.

Percherons are either grey or black. If the latter, they seldom have any white apart from a star or possibly a blaze on the front of the face. Though there may be a bit of white on a Percheron foot, the white legs of Shire and Clydesdale are not acceptable in the Percheron.

Today's Shire colours are black, brown, bay and grey. The blacks often have those sparkling white legs sported by some of the leading brewery teams. To the model enthusiast, black is probably an advantage, as a team of two or four blacks

may be all of the same intense shade, whereas the other colours vary, and so if perfectly matched present a slightly unreal appearance.

The Suffolk is always chesnut, spelt without the central 't'. A white blaze, shim or star is permissible, but there should be no white on a Suffolk's body. The chesnut may be one of seven shades, from mealy or very light to near black, but the model enthusiast is safe if the middle range of rich red or bright chesnut is chosen.

Shires and Clydesdales have feathery legs, while Suffolks and Percherons are clean-legged breeds. The tail of a Suffolk is always dressed long, whereas a Shire's may be shorter and sometimes shaven. But there is a growing tendency towards free flowing tails, and Percherons are usually shown with fairly long tails.

Among the vehicles, a dray is regarded as a four-wheel vehicle with seat attached. Thus brewery vehicles are generally termed drays, but the terms are open to different interpretations, as are rulley and waggon. The rulley is a flat-topped four-wheel vehicle with no seat, and is generally drawn by a single horse. A waggon may have a pole for two horses or shafts for one, though sometimes double-shafted waggons are made. Waggon design varies according to the county of origin, and each has a wealth of fascinating detail.

The Oxfordshire waggon has a convex curvature of rails over the rear wheels, as has the slightly smaller Berkshire type. Sussex waggons stand about 6 ft high at the back, $5^1/_2$ ft high in front and are nearly 14 ft long. The floor is often narrowed behind the front wheels to allow the wheels to lock round in a tight turning circle. Suffolk waggon wheels lock round into specially made recesses, while a narrow wheeled hooped waggon was made in Wiltshire and Gloucestershire, with very high rear wheels.

Waggon wheels are of four main parts. In the centre is the nave or naff, usually of elm though possibly of oak. From it are mortised the spokes, usually twelve in number and made of oak. They fit into the circumference, which is in segments of

Left *Oxfordshire waggon.*

Right *Cart or waggon lamp.*

hardwood, each segment or felloe taking two spokes. The whole is bound by an iron tyre.

Many model enthusiasts have told me that the wheels are the most difficult part to make. They can now be bought ready made, and it is no disgrace to do this. The model can then be completed and the next started. As more skill is acquired, another attempt at wheel making may be tried if desired, but it would be a shame for such a splendid hobby to become tedious in the search for perfection in every hand-made item. There is a vast amount of scope without making wheels.

Farm carts vary as much as waggons. They can be fitted with side boards, front boards and end boards, which enable a greater bulk of potatoes or turnips to be carried. They may have racks, or shelvings, fitted after removing the side and end boards. Hay and corn in the sheaf are carted with shelvings fitted. Fore and aft of the shelvings, racks or gaumers enable the load to be built without too much skill on the part of the loader. Ladders or racks are also fitted at the front of rulleys, but less frequently.

The only departure from these norms could be a piebald heavy horse, for while none of the main breeds accept the colour, it is depicted on old plates, and a good piebald is a striking animal. Whatever the type of horse used or vehicle copied, model making is a most satisfying hobby that gives hours of pleasure to a great many people.

Chapter 12
Decorated horses

PLAITING

Each of the four main breeds of British heavy horse has its own style of plaiting, used for the in-hand or breed classes, when the horse is not harnessed to a vehicle, but is being judged according to the breed standard. In the harness or turn-out classes, a rather different pattern of decorations is used.

For a Shire the mane is combed to one side of the neck, and a 'bass' consisting of three sections of ribbon and raffia is plaited into it. The bass is laid on the neck, just behind the ears. Only a proportion of the mane is incorporated, while the remainder is combed down the side of the neck. A flag, plaque or standard is incorporated every few inches or after a regular number of plaits. The object is to

Left *A whole host of items is necessary in preparing the big horses for show.*

Above right *Young dark bay Shire mare Granhurst Lisa (Colin Fry).*

Right *The neckband on this winning Shire mare enhances the length of the neck (David A. Guiver).*

Above *The height of the big horses is demonstrated by these aids to show preparation.*

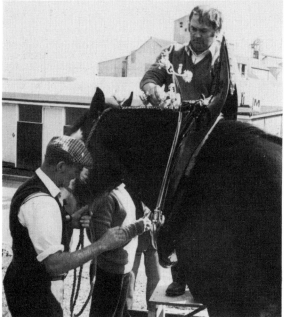

Left *The collar is decorated first. Early morning scene at the Royal Highland Show (Audrey Hart).*

Braiding a Shire calls for intense concentration.

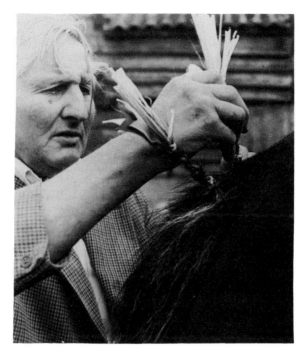

enhance the line of the neck, and if a collar is to be fitted, the plait ends further up the neck to allow room for it.

The Shire's tail is plaited round a 'jug handle', not usually copied by other breeds. One style of Shire dressing is the shaven tail, with the remaining tail hair plaited over it, but this abomination is intensely disliked by spectators, and the Shire Horse Society does not encourage the practice. Shaving began when tail docking was banned. In the old days the tail itself was shortened but quite an attractive length of hair remained. Some grooms did not like the full length tail and resorted to shaving to help prevent the reins becoming fast under the tail, and for added smartness, but it has nothing to commend it.

The better method is to take hair from either side of the top of the tail, and plait pieces about the thickness of a finger, incorporating raffia. On either side two rather thinner pieces are plaited, starting nearer the tail root, and using enough raffia to make them upright, like two pencils, with the raffia projecting at the top. The jug handle is tied to the first plait, and brightly coloured ribbons affixed just below it, dangling down some eight inches and clipped off in fish tail fashion. The rest of the hair is then combed down.

Horsemen north of the Border have their own styles of plaiting. Adult male Clydesdales, both stallions and geldings, are shown with decorated rollers topped with pom-poms. A roller is a girth strap to which the off rein is attached, preventing the animal swinging to his left and knocking his groom's head with his own.

Right *Clydesdale tail decorations on a yearling filly at the Royal Highland* (Audrey Hart).

Left *Showing at the trot.*

Below left *Mane decoration, Scottish style. Many hours' work and years of experience are needed* (Audrey Hart).

Eight pom-poms are used on top of the roller; three on either side and one at each end of the ridge. No one seems to know why eight are used, other than because the sizes readily obtainable just fit in that number. The pom-poms appear to add to the animal's height; Clydesdale stallions and geldings always look tall. In mares, stallions under two years old, and geldings shown in-hand, the neck is not plaited. 'Two wee standards on the tail' suffice in these classes.

The tail is combed out and parted, then each side parted again. Two bunches of raffia are then plaited into these two pairs, generally finishing with nine plaits in a well-endowed tail. When a horse has been rubbing his tail, the artist must make do with fewer.

'Soaping up' is done in some classes, using a ball of soft soap and working against the lie of the hair. The result is a sea of neat ripples over the whole body, adding to the appearance of bulk. But if the show day turns hot, 'soaped' horses soon seek a rubbing post.

The Diamond Roll and the Aberdeenshire Roll are peculiarly Scottish mane decorations. The former uses four harmonising colours, and the Aberdeen Roll two. The plaiter stands on a box with someone holding the horse's head up in show position. Many hours of practice are needed to perfect these arts. The finished effect is a combed-out mane with the plait resting just below the crest on the same side and running its length.

Preparation of a Suffolk horse for showing begins as in the case of the Shire, the forelock being brushed forward and tidied later. All the mane is brushed to one side of the neck, and the bass laid on top with its knob just behind the ears. Now comes the difference. In the Suffolk, all the mane is incorporated in the plait. The crest of a stallion is accentuated by plaiting high on the crown of the neck, but slightly lower for geldings and mares. The plait is very tight in all cases. Plaques, flags or standards are inserted at regular intervals as plaiting progresses. The forelock is not plaited, but held neatly in position by a ribbon tying it to the browband.

The Suffolk tail is encouraged to grow long and is combed out before plaiting. It is plaited right down to the end of the dock, and the remaining hair is then divided into three, plaited and turned up and secured along the tail.

Exhibitors of the black and grey Percherons use a combination of styles. While the mane is plaited in Shire fashion, taking in only part of the hair, the tail is plaited long. No loose hair is left anywhere on it, and the end of the brushed-out tail is plaited and turned up on itself, Suffolk style. A jug handle-type decoration may be used near the top of the tail. Percherons often have splendid tails, contrasting with the body colour, and the comparisons with other breeds above are for the sake of descriptive purposes, not to imply any lack of individuality. In fact, well-turned-out Percherons are at least the equal of any others.

HARNESS DECORATIONS

A heavy horse has a huge body area, most of which may be covered by decorations, and in some cases it is! The really skilled horse decorator does not aim merely for abundance, however. The decorations should enhance the horse's best characteristics, not disguise them. Decorations range from bunches of raffia in the tail to a whole range of brasses, bells and terrets. There are classes for the best-decorated animal, and in turn-out classes some brass is essential to be among the tickets.

It may be a surprise to learn that modern Scottish, and that means Clydesdale, decorations are far in advance of anything accomplished in the heavy horse's heyday. The decorated classes for heavy draught horses at the Royal Highland Show at Ingliston, Edinburgh, in late June, are a Mecca for heavy horse people.

Naturally earlier in the century some much larger classes were staged, with 72 in one class at a Coupar Angus event, but materials were then more limited; coloured paper, crepe and roses were the chief materials. Today plastic flowers are popular. They withstand Scotland's uncertain climate and may be used repeatedly. Eventually even plastic takes on a worn appearance and is replaced, for sparkling freshness is essential to catch the judge's eye amid such competition.

Only a fanatic would prepare for half the evening and then rise at 4 or 5 am on a misty showground, but that is how such perfection is achieved. The saddle bridge is the focal point, topped with wire frames holding an astonishing array of decorations. Mane, tail and saddle decorations must all match. The horse is paraded in harness but without a vehicle, and wears the high Scottish peaked

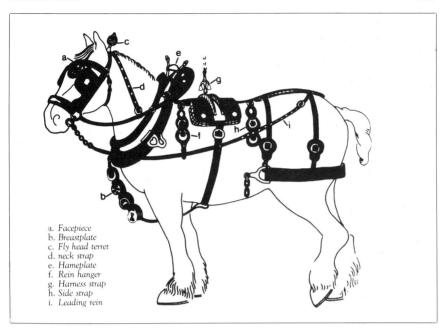

a. Facepiece
b. Breastplate
c. Fly head terret
d. neck strap
e. Hameplate
f. Rein hanger
g. Harness strap
h. Side strap
i. Leading rein

Above *The English harness decoration* (Terry Keegan).

Below *A highlight of the heavy horse year is the trade turnout class on Smiths Lawn, Windsor Great Park* (Colin and Janet Fry).

Above *Mr Barry Coffen of Winchester, Hampshire with the roan Clydesdale Jim (Colin Fry).*

Above right *Perfection. Main ring assembly at the Royal Highland's decorated harness classes (Audrey Hart).*

Below left *The 'bridge' over the saddle is the centre piece in Scottish harness decoration (Audrey Hart).*

Below right *Fly terrets between the ears were originally protective.*

collar, saddle, breechings, plough chains and belly band. A soft cloth protects the breechings below the tail till judging starts, so keen are the exhibitors to ensure perfection in every detail.

In the south of England, decorations reflect the warmer climate in the use of fly terrets whose original purpose was protective. Other horses wore ear caps or muffs to ward off the flies, but the team leader had to hear properly and wore a terret. Plumes are added to the terrets for show purposes, and may be made in multiples. A practical disadvantage is that when the flies are very busy, tormented horses shaking and nodding their heads may tangle the terrets in their neighbour's harness.

BELLS

The use of bells on horses is age-old, being used to give warning of approach by heavy horse teams over the past two centuries. Culley describes them in 1794.

> The vanity of many of the farmers in the south, in regard to their teams, is most extraordinary. I have, in Berkshire and that neighbourhood, several times met a narrow-wheel'd waggon, with six stallions, one before another; the first horse, besides having on a huge bridle, covered with fringe and tassels, enough to half-load a common Yorkshire cart-horse, has six bells hung to it, the next five, and so on to the last, which has only one; and it is really diverting to see with what a conceited air the driver struts and brandishes his long whip.

Had Northumbrian George Culley lived a century later, he might still have been surprised by the bells, for they are definitely a south-country acquisition. The reason, which Terry Keegan suggests, may well be that they are associated with waggon teams rather than carts, the former being so much more difficult to reverse in case of meeting another vehicle in a narrow lane, and being more widespread in the south. The trace horses, numbering two, four or even more, cannot help the backing process. Only the shaft or pole horses can do so, and

Stance is important, as this stallion shows.

obviously a load requiring six horses to move it forward cannot be backed by just the two wheelers. Hence the extreme care needed not to get into such a position.

There is in Hereford Museum a set of ten Robert Wells bells mounted on an elaborate wrought iron frame. Far too heavy to be readily carried by an individual horse, they were probably mounted on the waggon itself. Starting from the base the bells are in rows of four, three, two and one.

In *The Woodlanders*, by Thomas Hardy, is a marvellously descriptive passage about the passage of a loaded timber waggon. Each carter had a different tone to his set of bells, and could identify others approaching.

> The horses wore their bells that day. There were 16 to the team, carried on a frame above each animal's shoulders, and tuned to scale, so as to form two octaves, running from the highest note on the right or offside of the leader to the lowest on the left or nearside of the shaft horse...
>
> These sound-signals were still as useful to him [the carter] and his neighbours as they ever had been in former times. Much backing was saved in the course of a year by the warning notes they cast ahead; moreover, the tones of all the teams in the district being known to the carters of each, they could tell a long way off on a dark night whether they were about to encounter friends or strangers.

Dating from 1570, the Whitechapel Bell Foundry has become the world's foremost. Its records seldom specify horse bells, but on February 6 1841 there is an item which reads: 'Messrs Warners, To 8 Horse Bells, tuned musically — 18s 0d'.   Robert Wells of Aldbourne was among the best known for horse bells, but was taken over by the Whitechapel enterprise in 1825. One of its patterns was used in the 1960s to supply a set of sleigh bells for a fairground organ. The Robert Wells patterns covered 11 sizes, from 1 to 3½ in in diameter, and tuned to cover two chromatic octaves. Judging by the number of duplicated patterns, demand for these bells or rumblers must have been considerable.

Rumbler bells are cast with a small ball of iron given free play inside them. This playing against the enclosed hollow sphere of iron or bell metal gives a rumble rather than the clear ring of the open clapper type of bell.

Team bells for two pairs of horses or more still survive. Most were of the open mouthed clapper type, set in a rectangular frame. The bigger the bells, the fewer were fitted to each frame, which was fixed above the hames. In Herefordshire the bells were affixed to large iron hoops, one set being 3 ft wide and standing 2 ft above the hame fittings where it rested.

Metal hames were made with special fittings at their points to take bells. The spherical bell is also a protection; if a child happens to ride a big horse and falls forward on to a pointed hame, results are unpleasant. Hame top knobs or spikes were another form of decoration, but some of them were spiky. A brass head nail was used to secure some of the knob designs. A pair of crotal bells on a stem, one above the other, was slipped into staples on wooden hames, being secured there by a spring.

Either crotal or open-mouth bells were sometimes used in terret form, and Thacker of Walsall shows a whole range of these combined with plumes or terrets. The plume was the centre piece, and the bells suspended on their own framework either below, on either side, or both.

In the late 19th century a number of manufacturers produced bells incorporated in horse brasses. The brass itself was usually either circular (like a crotal bell) or open-mouthed, the bell being suspended where the tongue would fit. Double and triple bell brasses were also made, but did not become widespread.

Bells have been attached to martingales and face pieces, the martingale being specially suitable as the leather curves round the animal's breast, allowing the bells to hang clear, perpendicular and free.

It is surprising that bells were not used more often on farms. One Wolds waggoner told me: 'We used to set off at dawn on a foggy morning, some one way, some another, to find the horses in a 100-acre dale'. Bells on one or two leaders would surely have aided the quest. Bells on any animal can be a delight, as the beast's movements suffice to ring the tone, without further human aid.

Chapter 13
Horse brasses

Collecting horse brasses is an ideal hobby for the heavy horse enthusiast. There is
no need to own a horse; the collection in a private house can be an end in itself.
Nothing else adds more to the charm of house or cottage than a well-displayed
collection of brasses, whether on a wall or, as is so often the case, on the beams. If
those beams are of dark oak, so much the better. Their colour is the perfect
backcloth to brasses shimmering in the firelight, as publicans seeking to recreate
an atmosphere of Old England well know.

Brasses lend a 'period feel' to the most modern dwelling. They recall the age of
the heavy horse, of a more amenable pace of life, of pride in workmanship. They
are neat and enduring, have no maintenance problems, take little space, and do
not eat. So the person who has neither the time, space nor money to keep a Shire
or a Suffolk may still feel a real part of the heavy horse world through a collection
of horse brasses.

Capital outlay remains relatively low. Earlier and rarer brasses do indeed
command much money, into the hundreds of pounds for quite a small number,
but great satisfaction comes from the less expensive types, as will be outlined

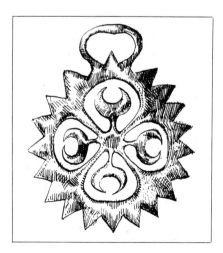

later. The available range is considerable, and each new collector adds to the manufacturer's outlets, inspiring still more brass designs. There is the probability of capital appreciation; quality brasses cast ten years ago are already showing a useful gain in value.

One pitfall for the brass collector is unfortunately modern. His pieces are easily stolen. If that happens they can seldom be readily identified, and disposal is easy. Public houses usually deter theft by fastening each brass permanently in its place, and if the home collector is in a district where this type of larceny occurs, he should follow suit. To have to keep such items under lock and key denies us one of the chief joys of possession.

Display brasses must be kept clean. Dull brasses give an air of neglect to their surroundings, in sharp contrast with the cheery welcome of shining brass. The more intricate the brass, the more cleaning it will take; a smooth brass is quickly wiped clean, whereas a crown set in a wreath of leaves is more time-consuming.

The third disadvantage is the fake. The most sought-after brasses are those actually used on horses, preferably pre-1914 and certainly pre-1939. As Lord Wigg (former chairman of the Horserace Betting Levy Board) said, 'In any society, even in Heaven, you will find somebody on the fiddle', and those engaged in faking brasses include some very skilled personages. Experience is the only sure guide and, even then, collectors are taken in. Imitators make the brass appear as though it rubbed against a horse's harness daily for a decade, when in fact it was burnished last month. New brasses on old straps are another blind.

One of the best guides to avoiding fakes is to be found in Peter Brears' *Horse Brasses*. Fakers have had most of this century in which to acquire their expertise, however, and the date on a brass is certainly no guarantee of its authenticity. Thousands of Queen Victoria Jubilee 1887 brasses were made for Queen Elizabeth II's Silver Jubilee in 1977!

There is one safe way. Start with modern brasses, and learn about them and

their feel. None is expensive and a specialised range may be accumulated without fear of paying above the odds. Over 30 different patterns were on sale in the Queen's Silver Jubilee year, 1977, yet few people set out to buy them all. Sold at around 45p to £4 apiece, a comprehensive collection is even now worth much more. Major events, such as national or regional ploughing matches, or heavy horse society centenaries, may well be marked by a special brass. The good ones are of fine workmanship and material and very well worth having.

THE HISTORY OF HORSE BRASSES

In the 18th century the affluent upper classes began to display their family crests on any driving vehicles reserved for special occasions. By the mid-19th century, middle class families painted intricate monograms on to their carriages. Until that time, the working heavy horse was disregarded as an object for ornament, just as it was by the majority of artists, commissioned to paint favourite hunters or racehorses, seldom Clydesdales or Suffolks.

Theories have been put forth that the horse brass was originally used to ward off spirits and 'the evil eye'. Later researches do not bear this out. I spent my childhood among farm workers who could remember well back into Victorian times, and none ever suggested such a connection, although they were firm believers in other old superstitions.

Horse brass manufacture coincided with the establishment of separate breeds and the stud book movement, though there is no direct link. A useful starting date is circa 1870, and for many years almost the only purchasers were the horsemen themselves. Farmers seldom bothered. The employed horseman spent his long working day with his charges, and his brief evenings in a dimly lit cottage. He had no wireless, no television, and the single oil lamp was barely sufficient for reading. It was, however, adequate to bring out and polish the few brasses that he could afford from near-subsistence wages. A reflection on the times is that, after the

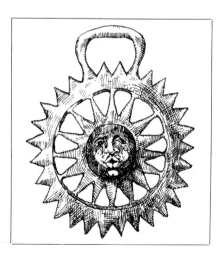

May Day parades each year, many brasses were pawned.

When a horseman moved to another place, he took his brasses with him. If a horse died or was sold, its successor wore the brasses. If landlord, employer or fellow worker died, the foreman's brasses would receive a very special clean and be used on the steadiest horses pulling the hearse.

The earliest brasses were probably made by tinkers and travelling people, fashioned privately for men on the farms through which they passed. From this primitive stage, horse brass manufacture became a cottage industry, and along the Yorkshire coast handmade brasses were reputedly made into the 20th century.

Larger-scale manufacture followed the harness trade. In early Victorian times Walsall had become an acknowledged centre, growing as numbers of work horses increased with more land under the plough and the greater needs of the British Army's cavalry and artillery regiments. Those concerned with the various stages of harness making, fellmongers and tanners as well as saddlers themselves, naturally congregated where the work was. Specialised craftsmen carrying on the trade in such accessories as spurs, rowels and buckles plied a craft that began in medieval times, and so had both tools and skill to make brasses.

The first brasses for general distribution were cast. Stanley Brothers of Walsall still produce brasses by this means, in which perhaps 15 separate patterns are made on one casting bench, and until 1914 the brasses were each provided with two studs or struts, projecting as rods from the rear of each, and used to hold the brass in a vice for hand-finishing, using a small file to leave a smooth outline. Each successive stage needed much labour and skill, and as demand rose, so the manufacturers sought new techniques.

Collectors who possess any of these early cast brasses have a prize indeed. Their fashioning was largely superseded in the late 1870s and 1880s through the technique of rolling brass into thin sheets which could then be easily cut to shape by dies mounted in heavy fly presses. The simple discs that emerged were passed

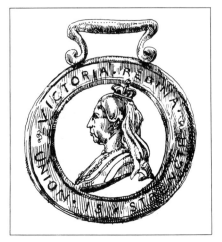

to individual craftsmen who used smaller dies with a variety of patterns. With such handwork no two brasses were exactly the same. Later refinements were to stamp the whole face in relief, using a variety of designs, and to add a central boss of coloured porcelain. Royal blue and crimson were the most popular colours, alone or in concentric rings.

We use the term 'brasses' for all these decorations, but nickel and German white metal also came in designs. The RSPCA, which holds as high a place in the horse brass fancy as it does in animal welfare, used a nickel coat of arms on a brass merit badge first introduced in 1895, and with aluminium merit badges from the 1930s.

SPREAD OF INTEREST

Not until the turn of the century did horse brass collecting cease to be the prerogative of the professional horseman and become of interest to others. Before World War 1 a few hobbyists were visiting country saddlers and buying what spare, used brasses they could. In the 1920s and '30s, more and more people took an interest in brasses, mainly through early or family associations with working horses.

At this time some notable private collectors were busy, foremost among whom was H.R. Carter, whose fine collection remains substantially intact in the Hull City Museums. Another was Dr John Kirk, whose practice at Pickering on the southern edge of the North Yorkshire Moors took him into the remote dales and across the flat and fertile Marishes plain. He collected about 600 brasses, and these may be seen at Castle Museum, York.

After World War 2, interest spread. The new collectors came from varying walks of life and from both town and country. Interest was such that by 1975 the National Horse Brass Society was formed, membership of which must rank as high priority for any novice collector. Through its auspices, members have been

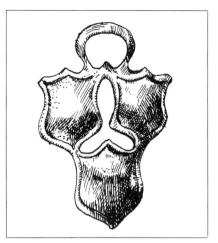 

able to study private collections not normally accessible to the general public.

With over 2,000 designs, and more coming out every year, there is ample scope for the enthusiast. Brewery brasses often incorporate a barrel, railway designs bring in a locomotive and the company's own lettering, while the Prince of Wales' ostrich-feather plumes have been popular for many years. Allusions to the land include plough, sack, sheaf and carter, which I at first took to be a shepherd, the apparent crook being in fact a whip. Country sports such as shooting and hunting are incorporated, the latter usually depicting a mounted huntsman jumping a gate.

Chapter 14
Rearing, breaking and stable management

FOALING

Most draught horses are spring-born. They arrive when freshening pastures stimulate the mare's milk supply, and mare and foal can spend their time out of doors, away from the dangers of infection inherent in old buildings. The Thoroughbred is foaled as soon after January 1 as possible, to give it advantage of growth when raced as a two-year-old. Such precise timing is less necessary with the draught horse, though if the foal is to be shown in summer or sold in autumn, a distinct advantage is gained from birth early in the year. A May foal is barely fit to leave its mother in October, let alone catch the judge's or buyer's eye.

Yet in horse breeding it is usually a case of getting the mare in foal when you can, rather than to any pre-arranged plan. The foal is carried for 11 months, and the mare should come in season again a few days after foaling. Horsemen find that this is usually the most successful time for conception, but if she does not hold to an early service the mare 'loses time', ie, foals later in the year on the next occasion.

If the birth takes place in February or March, the mare is given a clean loose box. A special foaling box may be provided, free from obstructions and dangerous corners. It will be fitted with a peep hole as many mares do not like to be under observation just before and during foaling. In fact, some have gone through a long breeding career and no one has seen them foal. One north country farmer was absolutely determined to see his favourite mare foal, a sight that had eluded him on her previous seven occasions. He spied through the peep hole every quarter of an hour right through the night and the mare showed none of the usual unease of labour. On his next 15 minutes' schedule, there was the foal, already shaking its head and ready to meet the world.

REARING THE FOAL

Once the foal is on its feet and has suckled, its attendants heave a huge sigh of relief, for a major barrier has been passed. There are so many things to go wrong with either dam or offspring, and the draught horse world has its quota of stories of care and attention lavished on an ailing foal, or one whose mother dies.

All horse people are quick to help one another in such circumstances; hunter, Thoroughbred and pony foals have been reared on draught mares, and vice versa.

Various proprietary mare's milk substitutes are now on the market, and are generally superior to older methods. Even so, a great deal of work is necessary by night and day. If the foal is reared at the end of it, the exhausted helpers feel amply rewarded. The value of the saved animal is of course a consideration, but it really boils down to love of animals and good old-fashioned stockmanship.

A Cumbrian Clydesdale breeder had a foal born, apparently normally. The mare was found dead the same day, so with his vet's help he set about rearing the foal. To complicate matters, the youngster contracted joint ill, a bacterial condition of the limbs, necessitating help rising to its feet. Finallly the foal was getting up itself and the battle now seemed won. Then it too was found dead. It had contracted a secondary infection to which it had no resistance. This sad story illuminates the pathos as well as the triumphs of draught horse breeding. That Clydesdale foal was a black filly with four white socks, already sold unseen for a large sum.

One story with which older horsemen regaled our youth concerned a Shire mare. She was walking to the field pulling an empty cart when one of the men shouted: 'Loose out the old mare, lads! She's going to foal!' The mare was unharnessed and delivered her offspring immediately on the verge. She was then re-harnessed, the foal popped into the cart and the journey resumed!

Ardennes mare and foal, with a stallion looking on, at Geoffrey Morton's Hasholme Carr Farm (Gavin Cole).

The foal soon learns to nibble grass.

True or not, it demonstrates an undoubted truth, that light work before foaling is of immense benefit to the mare. Foalings seemed more run-of-the-mill in the days when brood mares formed a sizeable part of the farm power. They were worked in chains almost up to foaling, though rarely in shafts, and certainly were not subjected to heavy backing or difficult loads. Today, when so many draught mares are kept for exhibition or purely for breeding, foaling troubles seem to occur more often. Exercise at pasture does not always prove sufficient.

If her foal is born early in the year, the mare will be fed on hay and concentrates. Once the grass comes, however, she needs little extra feed, for nothing stimulates the milk supply like spring grass. Permanent pasture is usually recommended. A new ley specially designed for rapid grass growth may prove too laxative, so that the mare's dung becomes loose and, in farming terminology, she 'scours'. When this happens the food is being incompletely digested, as proved by loss of condition in any 'scouring' stock.

The subject of the best grasses for horses deserves far more study than it has been accorded. Most of our knowledge is based on herbage mixtures of 50 years ago. Today's horse farmer must produce the maximum from every acre and generally, though by no means universally, this means from a ley. The breeder's aims in rearing a young horse are natural growth of bone and muscle, full development of the respiratory organs, strength of constitution and sound feet.

By combining adequate food with exercise and hygiene, these principles are achieved.

As soon as the foal can masticate it is encouraged to eat palatable hard feed, often a proprietary nut. The advantages are manifold. The foal gains extra nutriment to develop its frame; it is less liable to graze close to the ground, where most parasitic worms lurk; and it is ready to fend for itself when weaning comes. The foal becomes accustomed to the hand that feeds it and so begins its first association with man in a pleasant manner.

WEANING

The usual time for weaning is when the foal is five or six months old. A mare in foal again may benefit from the earlier date, but the practice of selling May foals at October sales does the draught horse industry little credit. Though arrangments are sometimes made for the pair to be re-united for a period after the sale, this is not always practical if buyer and vendor live far apart.

Weaning is best accomplished gradually. The pair is separated for longer and longer periods, until the final break is made. Both parties then benefit from other equine company. The 19th century horseman Captain Heaton stated: 'The colt should not be allowed to lose his foal's flesh' and this is the dictum to keep in mind. During its first autumn the foal is well fed, for three reasons. It must be compensated for the loss of its dam's milk; it is grazing autumn grass which, though green, has less feed value than spring or summer herbage; and the foal is at a period of high growth potential.

From about Christmas onwards, the shelter of either a field house or a straw yard is needed. If the former, the doors are better removed competely. The young horse then goes in and out as it chooses, without the tragic chance of a door blowing shut and imprisoning the stock for some time before the accident is noticed.

Show people aver that an out-wintered horse keeps its summer coat better and longer than a more pampered animal. With young draught animals, the ideal is shelter when needed, combined with a run on to sound pasture.

SECOND AND THIRD YEARS

If possible, the sexes are separated as the second year begins. Colts of potential stallion quality are given further assessment and the others are castrated to become geldings. Although colts increase less in height from one year to two years than in their first year, they thicken out tremendously, and their constitutions are formed. An abundant supply of good food is thus needed, though the ration may be less concentrated than during the first year.

Good permanent pasture usually suffices to start the second year, but a small feed from time to time ensures contact with man. The skilful owner accustoms his or her young horses to handling, and a horse that throughout its life may be caught through rattling a few nuts in a bucket is a great asset. Those that cannot are terrible time wasters and were one reason for the draught horse's demise in the 1940s and '50s. Young horses are generally better cared for than in the days when they were important sources of power and income. Anyone keeping a draught horse for fun naturally wants to spend time with it, otherwise the exercise is pointless.

The second winter is spent either in yard or loose box, or preferably on free-draining pasture with open shed attached. Hay and corn form the basic ration.

After its second birthday the young draught horse is approaching the stage of either work or breeding or both. Its feed must be ample in quantity and quality, and the amount that a young Shire of Clydesdale can put away is astonishing to those more used to ponies. Good pasture suffices during spring and summer, at the end of which the horse is about two and a half, and has almost reached its adult height. It will continue to fill out, however, perhaps up to five years old in the case of a late-maturing stallion.

There is nothing wrong with late maturers. They may outlast some of the brilliant foals, and the practice of awarding championships to foals or yearlings over the heads of mature animals can only be recommended in exceptional circumstances.

BREAKING

Though the term 'breaking' is widely used in the horse world, it is a misnomer. 'Training' is better; the aim is the sort of response and affection expected in the sheepdog world, not a submissive breaking of spirit.

The first stage is the halter, a head piece without a bit. Farm colts were often 'swung' on weaning, 'swinging' being the term for training to lead. The colt is fitted with secure head collar and the shank held by sufficient men to match the youngster's strength. The shank can be attached to an immovable object, but the danger of the colt hurting itself in its struggles is a real one.

Today more time is spent with foals, and the younger they learn the halter's purpose, the better. A Suffolk or Percheron foal a few days old is manageable by a single person, whereas after a few weeks it is not! If taught to wear a halter and follow the person holding the shank before its strength develops, the foal and also the groom are saved a deal of effort.

The best conceivable education is the show ring. If foals are to accompany their dams to summer events, and are shown themselves, they must be handled. In today's highly competitive world the judge cannot be expected to take much time over a foal that charges all over the place when the rest are under control. So the foal is taught to lead.

To reach the showground it must travel in trailer or horse box, to enter which it runs up the ramp alongside its mum. The lesson is invaluable. Easy boxing is an asset in any horse's character, and once taught the accomplishment is not lost. The foal's halter shank is thrown over its back, and in it trots alongside the mare. Time spent repeating the operation pays handsome dividends.

Then the judge will want to examine the foal in detail. For this to happen it must be quiet and accustomed to strangers. To be handled all over, to stand still, to have its teeth examined and its feet picked up is a definite advantage in either a show or a work horse. The show ring provides the early incentive for training,

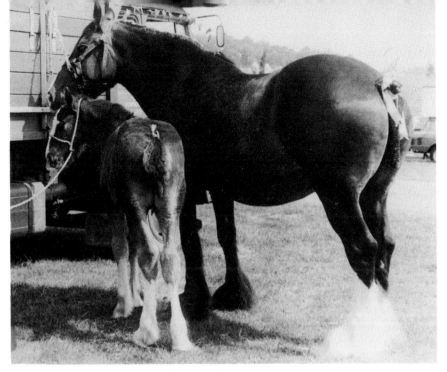

Shire mare and foal at a summer show (Audrey Hart).

otherwise the job tends to be delayed until too late. A foal that stands quietly to be groomed and have its feet washed is half broken.

BITTING

However well and frequently a young heavy has been handled during rearing, it faces one major barrier before it can be harnessed. It must be 'mouthed' or bitted — taught to accept a bit in its mouth.

Bits come in all shapes and sizes, and according to an old saying 'there is a key to every horse's mouth'. Most of the severe or intricate bits are designed to cure faults, usually man-made; it is the horse breaker's aim to ensure a soft and responsive mouth amenable to the lightest touches. Yet the acceptance of a piece of cold metal in its mouth is bound to be resented by the young horse, and time and patience are the first essentials.

The late Gerry Sowerby, from Lower Dunsforth, York, broke well over a hundred horses in his career. He stressed that many potentially quiet horses are ruined through improper and impatient mouthing. 'You simply cannot work to a timetable', he said. 'Ten to 13 weeks are the minimum from beginning mouthing to yoking for the first time in either chains of shafts.'

When he took in a strange horse, Gerry Sowerby tied it up in an airy stall and handled it for at least a fortnight, building up confidence. The youngster learned that handling over any part of the body was not to be feared and that having its feet picked up was mere routine. Obviously a horse that has been handled in this way since birth begins with a distinct advantage.

The next stage is to strap on approved breaking tackle, incorporating the mouthing bit. This bit is thick, with 'keys' in the centre whose object is to encourage the horse to chew them. The bit should rest on the bars or sides of the mouth and never be strapped tightly into the corners. At first an hour a day is allowed, extending gradually till the bit is left in all day after a week or more. Some horses turn sulky and refuse to play with the keys. They must be given more time until they do.

Sometimes a horse resents the bit and literally sets its teeth against it. Trying to force the metal against the front teeth is fatal. Finger and thumb should be inserted in the gap behind the front teeth, and the bit slipped in as the horse responds to the movement. Inserting the bit must become a simple routine, not an occasion for battle stations. The loriner's art with bits and bridles is basically the same whatever the class of horse and there is no fundamental difference between bitting a Shetland or a Clydesdale.

The next step is pillar reining. The horse is backed out of its stall, and then backed into it. The action of backing is itself a very necessary part of the draught horse's career. A rein is attached to each bit ring and thence to the pillar on that side. Though the reins are allowed a little play, the animal cannot move very far forward. It learns that a solid barrier is not necessary to control its movements.

The next stage is to work the youngster with 'long reins' attached to the breaking bridle. The mouth should be 'made' by this stage, so an assistant to hold the bridle should be unnecessary. The horse is driven round and round a field until it stops, starts and responds to the reins to move in either direction. Then journeys along tracks and quiet roads are undertaken, and finally among traffic.

Accustoming a young Shire or Suffolk to as many new and different situations as possible is an essential preliminary to showing. It is manifestly unfair to judges and fellow competitors, and dangerous to spectators, if an improperly schooled horse is entered. At the autumn foal sales some entries appear to have seen a halter for the first time on the previous day and their owners do no credit to the heavy horse world. While no one expects a foal to behave like an old stager, a degree of discipline is necessary in public places.

COMMANDS

The draught horse is driven by means of two sets of commands; rein and voice. It is accustomed to the reins gradually, as we have seen, by making its mouth accept and respond to the bit. Throughout all its training it is also taught to respond to the voice. The foal is taught that its owner's voice means kindness. It learns its own name, and in team work a horse that responds to its own and to no other name is an asset.

We were once chatting to a bevy of horsemen in Young's Ram Brewery stables, Wandsworth. Two or three stalls away stood Hercules, one of the big black geldings with four flashy white legs that graced the show team at the time. In the course of the conversation, a groom mentioned 'Hercules' in a normal voice. The horse immediately poked his head over his stall and looked towards his groom, giving a tremendous whinney. Such affinity comes from many hours of constant association, but it is a sure sign of mutual trust and kindness.

BREAKING TO HARNESS

Some time after its second birthday, the young draught horse is fitted with a collar. The fit must be correct, otherwise the youngster is uncomfortable and ill-disposed to give of its best. The first lesson is usually to pull a log or something similar of medium weight. The horse learns to lean into its collar, and after a few

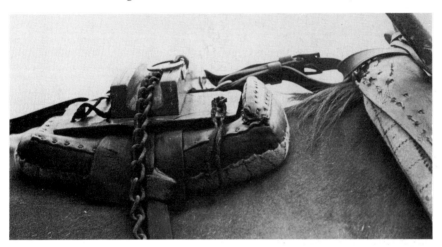

Above *Correct fit in the cart saddle is essential, otherwise chafing quickly occurs* (Audrey Hart).

Right *Strong chains are vital for working harness. Note the wooden hame strapped top and bottom, and fitting the collar snugly* (Audrey Hart).

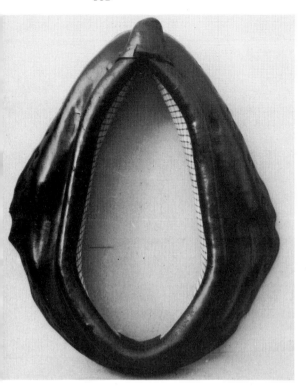
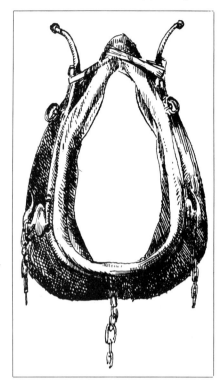

Above left *A nicely restored heavy horse collar* (Gavin Cole).

Above right *Standard English neck collar — carthorse.*

lessons it may be yoked between two steady 'old stagers' in an implement. Chain harrows are ideal, as a steady pull is required and if a mishap occurs and the horse plunges on to them damage is unlikely. Straight-tooth or chisel harrows could obviously cause injury if stepped on.

An ideal position for the novice is as middle horse in a yoke of three ploughing in line. This system is more usual in heavy-land districts, to reduce paddling on the top soil, for all three walk in the furrow. The first in single line in a three-horse team is termed the 'fore-horse', while the last (nearest the plough) is the 'thiller'. The middle horse is the 'body', and that is the learner's place.

TEMPERAMENT

In the 1920s a Vale of York farmer was cutting corn with the binder, when sickness and lameness reduced his team's strength. He and his horseman took a two-and-a-half year old filly, accustomed to nothing more than a halter, and yoked her between her mother and another old horse, the three abreast. She played her part in the binder for the rest of that day. Such animals are quite exceptional. Her owner-breeder knew all about her placid nature. More like her would further advance the working of draught horses.

Breeding for sound temperament has been sadly neglected. Top show horses are often spirited, and stallions are selected for colour, size and action, not because they are sensible and easily trained. Many leading stallions, especially Shires and Clydesdales, have never seen the inside of a collar. This is no new phenomenon. A century ago there was an outcry against show condition in Shires, and a very eminent breeder of those days said on the subject of fat: 'It is a matter of no consequence to anyone, save their owners, when second- or third-class horses are laden with blubber; but it is a national calamity when the best animals — those that ought to be the proud sires and dams of an ever-improving race — are stuffed with treacle and drugged with poisons in order to compete successfully with their inferiors.'

J. Albert Frost wrote in 1915: 'In past times working stallions could be found, and they were almost invariably good stock getters, but since showing has become popular it is almost a general rule to keep well-bred, or prize-winning, colts quite clear of the collar lest they should work themselves down in condition and so fail to please possible buyers on the look-out for show candidates.'

The position is even worse today. Between the Wars stallions might not work, but they walked. Their mile after mile through the rural lanes of Britain, six days a week for three months or so, sorted out the unfit. If a stallion's legs broke down he could not continue and so he got no foals to perpetuate the fault. Now the stallion either stands at home, where mares are trucked to him, or he travels his circuit in a motor wagon.

The late Robert Mitchell, who bred four Cawdor Cup winners (more than any other man) told me that the Clydesdales of his boyhood in the early days of this century were more intelligent and better natured. That was before the more intensive period of inbreeding to such horses as Baron's Pride, Baron of Buchlyvie and Dunure Footprint. Those mighty stallions left so many sons that inbreeding and the fixing of physical characteristics occurred. This fixing of type appears to have been accompanied by meaner natures, less placid and less intelligent than the former general run of farm horses. Mr Frome's brown mare, in the early Clydesdale volumes, is described as being 'as wise as a man.'

Another fundamental truth from J. Albert Frost states: 'The secret of training any horse is to keep it from knowing its own strength; therefore, if it is taught to lead before it is strong enough to break away, and to be tied up before it can break the headcollar by hanging back, it is obvious that less force is required.'

He adds a counsel of perfection, yet a perfectly attainable one that applies equally to all breeds: 'The Shire breeding farmer ought to be able to go into his field and put a halter on any animal required, from a foal to an old horse, and he can do this if they have been treated with kindness and handled from their early days.'

FEEDING

Rations for the heavy horse remain firmly based on grass in summer and oats and hay in winter. Various proprietary foods are now available, and barley and other cereals substituted for oats used as part of the concentrated ration, but the needs of herbivores such as the horse are fairly straightforward.

As the horse is not a ruminant, its feed differs markedly from cattle and sheep. One major drawback to the use of oxen in draught is not only the time they need to eat their midday meal, but the rest which follows while they chew the cud. The horse has a comparatively small stomach and must be fed 'little and often' when at work. The horseman's first task each morning while his team is stabled is to give a feed of corn, usually oats and perhaps some chaff or chopped hay mixed with it. This is done in a clattering and whistling fashion, so that the horses know what the grooms are about, and do not tread on them accidentally. 'The Old Squire' wrote of:

> The same glad cry of joyful hound,
> The whistling of my grooms,
> The clatter from the stable sounds
> Like music through my rooms.

A draught horse of average size (about 1,500 lb), should receive 10-12 lb oats, 8 lb hay, 10 lb oat straw and a few swedes or mangels. On medium work the oats are raised to 14-16 lb, hay to 16 lb and though roots are still fed, oat straw is cut out altogether. For continuous heavy work an even more concentrated diet is offered. Peas, beans, oats, maize and bran are mixed and fed at up to 20 lb daily, with 14 lb hay. The Liverpool vet Richard Reynolds, writing a century ago, outlined the rations of 200 cart horses under his care: 'Indian corn (maize) 10 lb: Beans or peas 5 lb: Oats 2 lb: Oatmeal or linseed 1.3 lb: Bran 2.1 lb: Hay 10.6 lb: Roots and grass 0.3 lb'.

'Maize, beans, or peas, with bran and cut hay, form the basis of the usual food allowance,' said Reynolds. 'The oats and linseed are used only for sick or delicate feeding horses. The oatmeal is made into gruel, of which each horse is allowed a drink on coming into his stable when the day's work is completed.'

Reynolds was in charge of a Liverpool stable, that great port opening on to the Atlantic trade routes through which so much American maize passed. Farmers of the period might use home-grown oats in lieu. A more modern substitute for oats is sugar beet pulp, a by-product of the sugar refining process. In feed value it is approximately equal to oats when assessed on dry weight, but on no account must it be fed dry to horses. Beet pulp must be soaked in water for 24 hours before feeding, taking up several times its own volume. Ruminants such as the cow or sheep can digest dry beet pulp; non-ruminants like the horse cannot. Stomach juices acting on the dry feed could prove fatal.

From May to October, little food other than good pasture is needed. When horses are working hard, as in harvest time, a supply of green tares, clover or lucerne is invaluable. The small quantities needed are easily mown with a scythe and are better and cheaper than offering precious hay.

After giving his team the first morning feed of corn, the groom pushes the clean bedding to the front of the stall ready for re-use, and brings his barrow to 'muck out' the rest. All this time he moves noisily so that the big horses are aware of his presence. Nailed boots are an advantage over wellingtons; creeping about the stable in the latter is to invite the dangerous alarm of a big horse suddenly aware of the unexpected. The hay ration is given, and then the groom goes for his own breakfast. In some stables it is the practice to put the collars on before breakfast, so that they are warming up ready for work.

Water is given before feeding, except when a horse is much over-heated. A drinking bowl is now usually fitted, with a means of cutting access on the rare occasions when that is necessary. Heavy horses can consume great quantities of water and carrying in buckets is unsatisfactory. A clean supply in the stable yard trough was the usual practice before water bowls were in general use.

Chapter 15
Shoeing the heavy horse

At one time a shortage of farriers threatened the heavy horse renaissance. Fortunately the Worshipful Company of Farriers, the Council for Small Industries in Rural Areas and kindred organisations have combined with heavy horse breed associations and improved the position considerably. Many farriers prefer a well-mannered heavy to the more flighty riding animals they may be called on to shoe. There is more foot to work on, and a really well-shod animal stands out among the rest.

Shoeing competitions for heavies are such a spectator attraction that they are now staged at several shows, including the Shire Horse Show at Peterborough and the Great Yorkshire Show, Harrogate. There is perennial satisfaction in watching the skilled manipulation of heated iron, the smell of hoof parings, the varying reactions of the great horses and the sleight of hand as each foot receives its sizzling metal protection.

'No foot, no horse' applies to all types, but to none more than the heavy breeds. Not only have they more muscle, but also increased friction between the hoof and the ground, and can therefore pull more.

Scientific tests have borne out the truth of another old horse saw: 'Weight is needed to move weight.' It is not only a question of well-tuned muscles and a willing spirit; the sheer weight of the heavy is pressed down to the ground through its hoofs, and so it can exert more pressure. In *Studies on the Draught Force of Horses*, 1958, Gustav Björck proved that a horse exerts the greater proportion of the pulling force on the toes of the shoes. He also found that the heavier the load, the more force is exerted on the hind limbs. Light loads are resisted almost equally between hind and fore legs.

Pulling tends to raise the fore quarters, and a heavy front end and the addition of a rider has been shown to increase draught ability. Perhaps those old-fashioned types of heavy horse of two centuries ago, with their low slung and rather coarse fore hands, were not so silly after all. The tall, upstanding horse has a higher point of draught, yet the lower the point of draught is the better as far as pulling is concerned, as tug-of-war teams well know.

When a shaft horse and trace horse were worked together, a boy or girl might ride the trace horse for fun. If the full load ever became bogged down, I can never recollect anyone telling the youngster to dismount and ease the burden on the

Above *Farrier watched by Bob Lomas, editor of Heavy Horse Magazine* (P. Styles).

Right *The forge at Vaux Brewery Sunderland cater for Percherons and Gelderlanders, a lighter harness breed.*

horses. Björck's studies show that this approach was the correct one, and that the additional weight of the rider was a help at that point. Obviously a heavy rider would tend to tire a horse. To verify these matters, Björck used strain gauges inside special shoes, together with a dynamometer.

TYPES OF SHOE

A horse at grazing requires no shoes, and in fact is better without them. Even so, the hoofs must be kept in trim, the amount of attention needed varying very much with the individual. A blue hoof is said to be harder than a white one.

For farm work, shoeing is generally needed. Here again it depends on the type of land; sharp, flinty soil causes far more wear on the foot. It was the practice on some farms to shoe the front feet only, shoeing 'all round' only when more road work was done. Flat, traditional shoes with toe and heel are usual for land work. In winter, 'sharp shoeing' with special projecting nails is carried out to give the horse a better grip. It is most essential for road work, when a horse pulling a heavy load on an icy surface could be wrenched down on to its knees with the effort generated, and suffer serious knee damage. In some regions the term 'slape shod' (slippery or smooth) shoeing is used, and a farm lad skidding on icy cobbles was told to go to the smith and be 'slape shod!'

Pulling competitions have engendered their own type of shoe. Pulling shoes are made to dig in, a whole range of methods being used to bring about this desirable state of affairs. Caulks and bars of various types and in various positions on the shoe are used, metal from old plough shares being one source. These pulling shoes are not suited to everyday work, being designed to cope with high initial thrust maintained over a short distance. As the competition area tends to give rather loose footing, it is essential that extra grip be obtained.

Shoes specially made for massive Clydesdale hoofs (Audrey Hart).

Another specialist shoe not generally used for everyday work is the show type. Bevelled shoes are popular, their rims sloping outwards at the same angle as the hoof, and thus making a wide foot seem even wider. Bevelled shoes are expensive, and are a major show ring cost.

Percherons and Suffolks have a more upright type of foot than the Shires and Clydesdales. A particular style developed north of the Border is used on Clydesdales, whose exhibitors aim for a very close action behind. This closeness of the hocks is accentuated by the shoes, and Clydesdale breeders outside Scotland may not be within range of a smith who specialises in the particular type of shoe required. The Scotch shoe is 'bumped back' in front so as to appear almost square. Fortunately, a number of shoes that fitted the leading stallions in the Clydesdale's heyday have been kept and give some indication of the huge frame they supported.

SURGICAL SHOEING

No two horses' feet are alike, nor is the way in which they walk. Some tend to walk with their hocks wide apart, in which case the inside of the shoe is made slightly thinner than the outside. Some walk on their heels and others on their toes, and the farrier is trained to note these points and to correct them in shoeing.

For a deformity or disease of the foot, special surgical shoeing may be necessary. A whole range of shoes was devised to keep horses at work, but these were very specialised, and some of the troubles they were designed to alleviate have now been bred out.

Chapter 16
Cross breeding

Although the heavy horse's main influence on human life and work is in its pure-bred form, it also contributes much as one parent of very useful cross-bred horses.

Either the heavy breed stallion or mare may figure in these breeding programmes. There is a saying in the horse world 'put blood on top' to indicate that when a Thoroughbred is used for crossing, it should be the stallion of that breed. Such a hypothesis does not always apply where heavy breeds are concerned. Among the best show jumping and eventing horses of the present time are a number with Shire or Suffolk stallion blood in them. Very good heavyweight hunters have been bred by Shire stallions on to the weedier type of Thoroughbred mares, sometimes putting the resulting cross to a 'blood' horse.

With the growing number of heavy breed horses to choose from, there is further opportunity for cross breeding. One class of horse always in demand is the heavyweight hunter, and that applies even when lighter and smaller animals are in recession. One stud where such a programme is regularly carried out is at Hollesley Bay Colony, near Woodbridge, Suffolk. The Colony Suffolks are used not only for showing and working but for producing hunter-type horses, some of which go as police horses.

Estate manager Mr John Bramley said: 'There's not much to choose financially between breeding Suffolk horses pure, and crossing them with a Thoroughbred. Pure Suffolk fillies sell better than Thoroughbred-cross fillies, but the half-bred geldings sell rather better than the pure Suffolk geldings.'

Buyers queue for the pure Suffolk filly foals at Hollesley Bay, despite the size of the stud. The Colony was able to set 24 Suffolks before Her Majesty Queen Elizabeth II in Gloucestershire in 1978, on the occasion of the Prison Service Centenary. The two Suffolk stallions at Hollesley Bay for the 1983 season were Parham Rufus, foaled in 1973, and the two-year-old Colony Timber by Marshland Baron. Besides the pure Suffolk mares there are some half-breds and three-quarters breds.

A successful three-quarter Thoroughbred/one-quarter Suffolk was Colony Lyric, whose 1978 foal was a dark bay seven-eighths Thoroughbred by Long Close. Lyric began her show career as a Best Hunter Brood Mare at Framlingham in 1978, and her foal the next year was the chesnut Red Lady, sold for £520 at the Hollesley Bay draft sale in October 1982, a time of depressed prices. Red Lady's sire was the Hunter Improvement Society stallion Red Canute. At the same sale Lyric's two-year-old daughter Solitaire, by another HIS stallion, King Willow, realised £750. Colony Nimble was a mare of similar breeding to Lyric, but she was put to the Suffolk stallion Parham Rufus, and bred a good colt foal.

The Suffolk's clean legs are an undoubted advantage in breeding riding horses, its chesnut colour less so. There is a prejudice among many horse people against chesnut as a colour, but that hardly seems logical when it stems from the generally admirably tempered Suffolk.

There are now sufficient pure Shire mares for a proportion to be used for crossing. At Little Ladbrook, Tamworth-in-Arden, Warwickshire, Arthur Lewis had half-bred and three-quarters-bred horses as well as his registered Shires. One lovely one-quarter Shire/three-quarters Thoroughbred made a superb heavy-weight hunter, and the Shire's hairy legs have disappeared in the process.

HARNESS HORSES
Another class in perpetual short supply is the powerful, tall and active harness horse. In the ten years up to 1882, almost 200,000 horses were imported into the United Kingdom, and most of these were for harness work. In 1898 Sir Walter Gilbey was lamenting Britain's dependence on imported carriage horses, when the proper stamp of animal could readily be bred at home. He was echoing a report by Mr E. Greene MP a quarter of a century earlier, giving evidence before the House of Lords' Horse Breeding Commission: 'I think that harness horses are really the most scarce animals; that is to say, a carriage horse, a phaeton horse or a horse to drive in a dog-cart. The qualifications for a hunter are not of the same description. With a hunter, men put up with a good deal. A horse that will jump is called a hunter, and people manage to find horses in that way. But for a harness

A pair of cross-bred draught horses. Note the semi-peaked collar typical of parts of the north of England and less pronounced than the Scottish full peak.

horse you want a certain amount of power and shape to fill the eye, and they are very difficult to get.'

The breeder's choice of a sire inevitably falls on a Thoroughbred if one be available, said Mr Greene, and the Thoroughbred has not the trotting action necessary in a harness horse. He has been bred to gallop, not to trot, and his progeny will resemble him. Mr Greene concluded that nothing is so valuable as a horse that steps well, and that a Thoroughbred does not often do.

Today there is a growing need for ride-and-drive animals, and a proportion of heavy bred blood can be an advantage. The Hackney/heavy horse cross is often admirable. It is less often seen these days, partly because there are so few Hackneys around compared with Thoroughbreds.

One that really took my eye was at the Alneland dispersal sale of Shires in 1981. A Hackney/Cob mare had broken out, as mares will, and been served by the Shire stallion Ryefield Select. Her colt foal was a beauty. The mare was then legitimately mated to the Hackney stallion Manorside John.

One of the finest four-in-hands in North America is a team of black Clydesdale/Hackneys, mainly with white socks. Shown on the 1981 Mischka Driving Calendar, they are pulling a Brewster park drag with eight passengers, and really leaning into their collars. They are admirably matched, as cross-breds often are.

Sir Walter Gilbey at the turn of the century extolled the virtues of the Hackney as a crossing sire. 'It is not, surely, too much to ask breeders to admit that the horses got in England by Hackneys from judiciously chosen mares are likely to be at least as good as horses got by Hackneys in France or Hungary? The breeding grounds of these countries are not superior to ours, nor do they possess any great climatic advantages over those of England.'

Such an appeal is equally applicable today, even allowing for the geographically uneven spread of really high quality Hackney stallions. Some who remember the

Percherons make ideal driving horses when crossed with a lighter breed. These greys are Percheron × vanners, seen at Beamish Horse Trials, County Durham (Gavin Cole).

old type of Hackney regard a proportion of modern entries as 'putting their foot down where they picked the last one up!'

The big mares known in the trade as vanners are also recommended by Sir Walter as suitable for the purpose. The vanner is not a breed but a type, and often contains a proportion of Shire, Percheron or Clydesdale blood.

One instance where the heavy breed stallion has done more harm than good is as a cross on pony mares. The resulting animals lost pony quality, for the pony has characteristics of nimbleness, intelligence and thriftiness that mark it from the horse. Travelling Clydesdale stallions were used on Dales pony mares when mechanisation spread tardily to the Durham and Yorkshire dales. The machinery designed for level lowland rather than steep upland needed bigger horses to pull it. So farmers tried crossing their ponies of 14.1 or 14.2 hands to Clydesdales, partly because the latter were readily accessible on their rounds. The result was a raw-boned, coarse animal that might serve an immediate purpose but did not improve the stock.

MULES

Another major cross-breeding use of heavy breeds is in mule production. In the United Kingdom, mules have never become as widespread as in the USA, where in 1920 there were almost five and a half million of them. This was an increase from 2,209,769 in 1910, and even in 1930 USA farmers still used 5,375,000 mules. Two thirds were in the nine Cotton Belt States, where almost three and a half million mules were used, plus almost two million horses. In 1948 there were still over two and a half million mules in the USA, and 1,600,000 in 1954. During the Boer War, export figures shot up, and in 1900 alone 43,369 mules were exported from the USA, with the astonishing total of 105,000 for the three years 1900-02.

The evenness of a large mule team is always its characteristic feature. The mares

Miniature cart horses. Dales ponies were the chief source of power on upland farms in Durham and North Yorkshire.

Pack horses were common before roads were improved. The modern version is seen here with game panniers as once used on the Raby Estate, County Durham.

from which they are bred may show great dissimilarity, but brown or black mules of very similar type are produced. Professor Hagedoorn, in his classic *Animal Breeding*, writes: 'It is astonishing to see the enormous variety between the mares and the uniformity in the mule foals, at any of the larger markets where mule foals are bought and sold. The mares differ as much as horses can possibly differ; the mules look as if they had been turned out by machinery.'

The fact that mules are infertile is too well known to coment on, but in fact a tiny proportion does breed, mainly the mares. Hagedoorn propounds another of his very practical ideas: 'It would certainly be possible to utilise the fertile foals from fertile mule mares to start a breed of mules that would be fertile and would free the breeders from the continued species-cross. In such countries (where horses do not stand the climate or the local parasites) breeding back the occasional fertile mare mule to horses would give the starting-point for a local breed of horses that would be adapted to the adverse local conditions. This is work that should be undertaken by Governmental experimental stations.'

Fashions have changed in mules as among other things. The big blacks and greys once dominated American show rings and gained high prices; now sorrels dominate. One reason is the upward surge of the blond Belgian horse in America. Mated to a red jack, the resulting mule with its attractive sorrel shade scales 1,400 lb to 1,600 lb, is of good temperament, and equally at home in the show waggon or the plough.

The general form and appearance of the mule should resemble those of the horse, and the same points of perfection are sought by judges. Height varies from 12 to $17^1/_2$ hands or even more, and weight from 600 to over 1,600 lb. Mules may be ridden as well as driven, and a smart, alert animal with a long, free stride at the walk, and a snappy, balanced trot, is sought.

With the four main heavy horse breeds firmly re-established in Britain, an interest in mule breeding may be about to take off, and is the very thing for those who like something different. A sorrel mule would undoubtedly attract enormous interest, but the necessary red jack mules would be a prerequisite. There is no reason why sorrel mules should not be bred from Suffolk or Suffolk-cross mares, and be worth a lot of money.

In 1962 carefully synchronised tests were carried out on two pairs of mules and two pairs of horses, of comparable fitness. The results are illuminating:

	Two horse pairs	**Two mule pairs**
Temperature rose by	5% to 40.2%	5% to 38.5%
Pulse rate rose by	149% and 116%	55% and 59%
Respiration rose by	157% and 154%	62% and 66%

During rest periods, the mules returned more quickly to normal. This is scientific backing for the practical horseman's knowledge that mules withstand heat better than horses.

Of the millions of mules that have served man down the ages, among the best known are the Death Valley teams. In the 1880s, William T. Coleman organised 20-mule teams to haul borax out of Death Valley, California, travelling a 165-mile route to the railhead at Mojave. In this hot, waterless region it was essential for the teams to haul their own supplies. Thus to the two freight waggons each

Ontario tunnel mule train (Jerry R. Springer).

weighing 4 tons, and loads of up to 10 tons, was added the water carrier for 1,200 gallons. That is 12,000 lb of water — more than 5 tons at the start. Each waggon was 16 ft long and its rear wheels were 7 ft in diameter. From 1883 the mules hauled more than £20 million worth of borax from the valley, without a breakdown.

When mules were commonplace, they were found in three main classes. Draught mules were the biggest, resulting from Mammoth Jacks on draught mares. The Mammoth Jack was an American evolvement from the fusion of some of the best French and Spanish jacks. The cotton mule came from a medium-sized jack and the utility farm mare or a lighter mare. Smallest were the mine mules, tough and wiry and well able to work underground.

Most American draught mules are now bred from good Belgian or Percheron mares, the most readily available breeds. Sired by Mammoth Jacks, these mules stand fully 15 to 16 hands high. While draught mules predominated in the north, cotton mules found more favour in the south, where cotton was grown. Both parents being smaller, the mules were suited to mountain riding and packing, as well as for inter-row cultivations in the cotton fields.

As with horses, the lighter ones tend to be more temperamental, but mule drivers insist that their charges are more responsive if properly handled, and that the really nasty or stubborn ones are man-made.

In circa 1000 BC Homer described the advantages of the mule over the ox for deep ploughing, and for hauling timber from forests, a task for which its value has been acknowledged by succeeding generations. The Roman Columella wrote extensively on mule breeding. The animal was so important to the Romans that they termed their veterinary works *mulomedicina* (mule medicine).

Mr Robert Way at Burrough Green, Newmarket, Suffolk, bred a mule foal from a Thoroughbred mare by a Poitou jack, but sadly lost it from grass sickness. He believes that the shortage of suitable jacks is the main limiting factor on mule breeding in Britain. He points out that, though most mules are gentle and affectionate, a bad one is worse than any horse. A mule can kick in any direction, and its front end is more dangerous than its rear. One had the habit of trying to get a man down with its teeth and then jumping on him.

Despite such eccentricities, the mule has several advantages over the horse as a draught animal. It will live longer, and if not overworked when young may have almost double the active life of an average draught horse. It has a knack of fitting into a large team without difficulty. Alexander the Great's funeral carriage was drawn by 64 mules. A 40-mule team drawing an American combine harvester has been driven by a 15-year-old boy. The mule has hard feet, so its shoes stay on better, if it needs them, and it consumes less and coarser food than the horse.

Appendices

1 Local hiring societies

A stallion hiring society is formed by a group of breeders in a particular area. They appoint a committee to select the type of stallion deemed most suitable for the majority of members' mares. The committee visits a number of stallion owners' studs and strikes a bargain to hire the one they favour for the season. Usually this is a straight fee, but is sometimes connected to the number of mares served.

The hiring society appoints a groom who stables the horse at a central point and takes him round the district periodically, usually in motor transport these days. Members pay a set fee per service and the stallion returns to his owner at the end of the season.

Mobberley & District Shire Horse Society Secretary: F.R. Marshall Esq, 36 Hawthorn Avenue, Wilmslow, Cheshire.

Yorkshire Shire Horse Society Secretary: W.H. Chambers Esq, Trinity House Farm, Swanland Dale, North Ferriby, Humberside.

Derbyshire Agricultural & Horticultural Society Secretary: B.G. Daykin Esq, 17 Chestnut Avenue, Mickleover, Derby.

Great Eccleston Shire Horse Society Secretary: T. Kay Esq, 2 Park Lane, Wesham, Nr Kirkham, Preston, Lancashire.

Montgomeryshire Entire Horse Society Secretaries: Morris, Marshall & Poole, Coach Chambers, Welshpool, Powys.

Wisbech Shire Horse Society Secretary: R.K. Reeve Esq, Agricultural House, 33a Alexandra Road, Wisbech, Cambridgeshire PE13 IHS.

Abergele & District Shire Horse Society Secretary: H. Thomas Esq, JP Garnedd, Llanfairfechan, Gwynedd.

Lincolnshire Shire Horse Association Secretary: B.A. Neave Esq, School Lane, Grayingham, Lincolnshire.

North Yorkshire Heavy Horse Society Secretary: A. Jenkins Esq, East Side Farm, Staintondale, Scarborough, North Yorkshire.

Wessex Shire Horse Hiring Society Secretary: Mrs G. Williams, High Noon, Village Hall Lane, Three Legged Cross, Wimborne, Dorset.

South West Yorkshire Shire Horse Hiring Society Secretary: A.K. Beaumont Esq, 22 Harwood Crescent, Morgate, Rotherham, York S60 3BW.

Lichfield Shire Horse Society Secretary: R.F. Schoffman Esq, St Mary's Chambers, Lichfield, Staffordshire.

2 Shows with Shire classes

March
National Shire Horse Show,
Peterborough.

April
London Harness Horse Parade (always
takes place on Easter Monday).
Nefyn Show, Gwynedd.
Cadnam Country Fayre, Hampshire.

May
Leicestershire County Show.
Newark & Nottinghamshire Agricultural
Show, Newark, Nottinghamshire.
London Horse Show.
Pageant Of The Horse, Doncaster
Racecourse, South Yorkshire.
Royal Windsor Horse Show, Windsor,
Berkshire.
Shropshire & West Midlands
Agricultural Show, Shrewsbury.
Devon County Show, Exeter.
Staffordshire County Show, Stafford.
Heathfield & District Agricultural
Show, Sussex.
Otley Show, West Yorkshire.
North Wales Show, Gwynedd.
Montgomeryshire County Show, Powys.
Hertfordshire Show, St Albans.
Derbyshire County Show.
Warrington Horse Society Annual
Spring Bank Holiday Show.
Woodhall Spa & District Agricultural
Show, Lincolnshire.

June
Suffolk Show, Ipswich.
Royal Bath & West Show, Shepton
Mallet.
Deeping Show, Peterborough.
Messingham Show, South Humberside.
Royal Cornwall Show, Wadebridge,
Cornwall.
South of England Show, Ardingly, West
Sussex.
Aberystwyth & District Agricultural
Show, Dyfed.

Honley Agricultural Show, West
Yorkshire.
Gorefield Show, Wisbech,
Cambridgeshire.
Thorne District Show, South Yorkshire.
Three Counties Show, Worcestershire.
Essex County Show, Chelmsford, Essex.
Whittlesey Show, Peterborough.
Cheshire County Show.
Lincolnshire Show, Grange-de-Lings,
Lincoln.
Putney Show, London.
Mid Southern Counties Show,
Hampshire.
Letchworth, Baldock & District Riding
Club Breed Show, Hertfordshire.
Hillingdon Show, Buckinghamshire.
Royal Norfolk Show, New Costessey,
Norwich.

July
Winterton Show, South Humberside.
Seaton Ross Show, York.
The Royal Show, Stoneleigh,
Warwickshire.
Pudsey Borough Show, West Yorkshire.
Market Bosworth Agricultural &
Horticultural Society Annual Horse
Show, Staffordshire.
Great Yorkshire Show, Harrogate,
North Yorkshire.
Kent County Show, Detling, Maidstone.
Alrewas Show, Staffordshire.
Swansea Valley Agricultural Show,
West Glamorgan.
Newport Show, Shropshire.
Snaith Show, Yorkshire.
Spilsby Heavy Horse Show,
Lincolnshire.
Great Eccleston & District Agricultural
Show, Preston, Lancashire.
The Hanningfield Show, Essex.
Ashby de la Zouch Show,
Leicestershire.
Royal Welsh Show, Powys.
East of England Show, Peterborough.
Royal International Horse Show,
London.

Littleport Show, Cambridgeshire.
Woolley Horse Show, West Yorkshire.
Pwllheli Show, Gwynedd.
Ryedale Show, North Yorkshire.
Royal Lancashire Show.
Nantwich & South Cheshire Show.
New Forest Show, Hampshire.
St Helens Annual Show, Merseyside.
Hull Show.
Leek & District Show, Cheshire.
Heckington Show, Lincolnshire.
Abergavenny & Border Counties Show, Gwent.
Oswestry & District Agricultural Show, Shropshire.
Llandyrnog Horse Show, Clwyd.

August
Harewood Show, North Yorkshire.
Nevern Show, Dyfed.
Bakewell Show, Derbyshire.
Southsea Show, Hampshire.
City Of Manchester Show.
Brecon County Show, Powys.
Canwell Show, West Midlands.
Penmorfa & District Show, Gwynedd.
Garstang Show, Lancashire.
Essex Tradesman's Show.
Sykehouse Show, South Yorkshire.
Anglesey County Show.
Ashover Agricultural & Horticultural Show, Derbyshire.
Great Christchurch Show, Dorset.
St Mellons Agricultural Show, Gwent.
Okehampton Show, Devon.
United Counties Show, Dyfed.
Penryn Agricultural Association, Cornwall.
Halifax Show, West Yorkshire.
Lancaster & Morecambe Agricultural Society, Lancashire.
Eglwybach Show, Colwyn Bay, North Wales.
Fillongley Show, Coventry.
Oldham Summer Show, Oldham, Lancashire.
Pembrokeshire County Show, Dyfed.
Denbighshire & Flintshire Agricultural Society Show, Clwyd.
Ashbourne Show, Derbyshire.

Bedwellty Agricultural Society Show, Gwent.
Llanrwst Show, Gwynedd.
Goosnargh & Longridge Agricultural Show, Lancashire.
Mid-Somerset Show.
Egton Horse & Agricultural Show, North Yorkshire.
Merioneth County Show, Gwynedd.
Burton, Milnthorpe & Carnforth Show, Cumbria.
Poynton Show, Cheshire.
Mobberley Shire Horse Society in Conjunction with Poynton Show, Cheshire.
Greater London Horse Show, Berkshire.
Kenilworth Show, Warwickshire.
Wentworth Show, Yorkshire.
Edenbridge & Oxted Agricultural Show, Kent.
Moorgreen Show, Nottingham.
White Horse Show, Uffington, Oxfordshire.
Alton Agricultural Show, Hampshire.
Woolton Show, Liverpool.
Walsall Shire Horse Show, West Midlands.

September
Bucks County Show.
Sheffield Show, Yorkshire.
Alresford Agricultural Show, Hampshire.
Orsett Horticultural & Agricultural Society Show, Essex.
Yesterday's Farming, Somerset.
Kington Show, Herefordshire.
Henley Agricultural Show, Oxfordshire.
Chertsey Agricultural Association Annual Show, Surrey.
Penistone Agricultural Society Show, Sheffield, Yorkshire.
Rotherham Show, South Yorkshire.
Thame Show, Oxfordshire.
Newbury Show, Berkshire.
Wisbech Shire Horse Society Show & Sale, Cambridgeshire.
The Midlands Shire Foal Show & Sale, Derby.

October

British Isles Horse & Tractor Ploughing
  Championships &Cruckton
  Competitions, Shropshire.
Horse of the Year Show, London.
Brailsford & District Ploughing &
  Hedgecutting Society Annual Match,
  Derby.
Great All England Ploughing Match,
  Berkshire.
North West & Wales Shire Foal
  Society Sale, Crewe.

Unclassified dates

Abergele & District Shire Horse Society,
  Gwynedd.
Burnley Agricultural Society,
  Lancashire.
Great Northern Agricultural Show,
  Lancashire.
Northern Heavy Horse Show & Sale,
  North Yorkshire.
Sandwell Special, West Bromwich, West
  Midlands.
Tottington & District Horse Show Ltd,
  Lancashire.

3   Shows with Clydesdale classes

January
Glasgow Foal Show.

February
Aberdeen Spring Show.

April
National Stallion Show, Glasgow.
Beith Show.
Ayr Show.

May
Royal Ulster Show, Belfast.
Neilston Show.
Fife Show, Leven.
Dalry Show.

June
Royal Highland Show, Edinburgh.
Central & West Fife Show.
Houston Show.
Scottish Central Show, Stirling.

July
Banchory Show, Aberdeenshire.
Kelson Show.
Doune & Dunblane Show.
Braco Show, Perthshire.
Angus Show, Arbroath.
Ryedale Show, Yorkshire.
Echt, Aberdeenshire.

New Deer Show, Aberdeenshire.
Drymen Show, Stirlingshire

August
Perth Show.
Turriff Show, Aberdeenshire.
Nairn Show.
Black Isle Show, Ross-shire.
Stewartry Show.
Biggar Show.
Kinross Show.
Keith Show.
Peebles Show.
Moffat Show.
Wigtown Show.

September
Strathaven Show.

October
Kilmarnock Foal Show.
Lanark Foal Show.
Wigton Horse Sale, Cumbria

November
Scottish Agricultural Winter Fair,
  Edinburgh.
Cupar Foal Show.
Stirling Foal Show.
Drymen Show, Stirlingshire.
Wigtown Show, Stranraer.

4   Shows with Suffolk classes

April
London Harness Horse Parade (always takes place on Easter Monday).

May
Woodbridge Horse Show, Suffolk.
Loddon Horse Show, Norfolk.
South Suffolk Show, Bury St Edmunds, Suffolk.
Hadleigh Show.
Soham Show, Cambridgeshire.

June
Suffolk Show, Ipswich.
Essex Show, Chelmsford, Essex.
Letchworth, Baldock & District Riding Club Show, Hertfordshire.
Mid Southern Counties Show, Hampshire.
Royal Norfolk Show, New Costessey, Norwich.

July
Crowland Show, Peterborough.
Royal Show, Warwickshire.
Tendring Hundred Farmers Club Show, Manningtree, Essex.
Southampton Show.
Great Yorkshire Show, Harrogate, Yorkshire.
Framlingham Show, Suffolk.
East of England Show, Peterborough.
New Forest Show, Hampshire.

September
South Somerset Agricultural Preservation Club, Shepton Mallet, Somerset.
Southern Counties Heavy Horse Association Ploughing Match and Show, Hampshire.

5 Shows with Percheron classes

May
British Percheron Show, Cambridge.
Newark & Nottinghamshire County Show, Newark.

June
Royal Norfolk Show, New Costessey, Norwich.
Suffolk Show, Ipswich.

Essex County Show, Chelmsford.

July
Royal Show, Stoneleigh.
Great Yorkshire Show, Harrogate.
East of England Show, Peterborough.

6   Waggon types in each county

The counties which are referred to in this list are those which were in use at the time when waggons were prevalent on the roads, before the amalgamations and boundary changes of more recent years.

Bedfordshire Hertford, Rutland, South Midlands Bow Waggon.
Berkshire Waisted Wiltshire, South Midlands, Surrey.
Buckinghamshire South Midlands, Hertfordshire.

Cambridgeshire East Anglian, Rutland.
Cheshire Waggons not now found. Stafford type probably found in 19th century.
Cornwall South-Western Bow and trolleys on larger farms.

Cumberland Waggons unknown.
Derbyshire Lincolnshire.
Devon South-Western Bow.
Dorset Dorset Box, Dorset Bow, South-Western Bow.
Durham No waggons.
Isle of Ely East Anglian, Rutland, Hermaphrodite.
Essex East Anglian.
Gloucestershire South Midlands Spindle-sided Bow, Panel-sided Bow, Hereford.
Hampshire North-West Hampshire, Dorset Bow, Surrey.
Hereford Hereford Panel-sided, Hereford Plank-sided, Trolleys.
Hertfordshire Hertfordshire, South Midlands.
Huntingdonshire Rutland.
Kent South-Eastern Box.
Lancashire No farm waggons.
Leicestershire Lincolnshire, Rutland, Staffordshire.
Lincolnshire Lincolnshire, Hermaphrodites.
Middlesex No waggons.
Norfolk East Anglian, Hermaphrodites.
Northamptonshire Rutland, South Midlands.
Northumberland No waggons.
Nottinghamshire Lincolnshire, Hermaphrodites.
Oxfordshire South Midlands.

Rutland Rutland, Lincolnshire.
Shropshire Shropshire.
Somerset South-Western Bow, Wiltshire, Dorset Box.
Staffordshire Staffordshire.
Suffolk East Anglian.
Surrey South-Eastern Box, Surrey.
Sussex South-Eastern Box.
Warwick South Midlands Bow, Rutland, Staffordshire.
Westmorland No waggons.
Isle of Wight Wiltshire.
Wiltshire Wiltshire.
Worcestershire Hereford Plank-sided, Trolleys.
Yorkshire Yorkshire, Trolleys, Lincolnshire.
Anglesey Denbighshire.
Brecon Radnorshire.
Caernarvon Occasional Denbighshire type.
Cardigan No waggons.
Carmarthen Occasional Glamorgan type.
Denbighshire Denbighshire.
Flint Denbighshire.
Glamorgan Glamorgan.
Merioneth Montgomeryshire.
Monmouth Hereford, Glamorgan.
Montgomery Montgomeryshire.
Pembroke Occasional Glamorgan type.
Radnor Radnorshire.

7   Places to visit

Intending visitors are advised to check dates and times of opening before making a special journey.

Courage Shire Horse Centre, Maidenhead, Berkshire. Museum of English Rural Life, University of Reading, Whiteknights Park, Reading, Berkshire (*Reading 85123 ext 475*).
Farmland Museum, 50 High Street, Haddenham, Ely, Cambridgeshire (*Haddenham 55159*).
Farm Museum, Mawla Well, Mile Hill, Redruth, Cornwall.
North of England Open Air Museum,

Beamish Hall, Beamish, Stanley, County Durham (*Stanley 33580 and 33586*).
Court House Museum, Hawkeshead, Cumbria (*Kendal 22464*).
Devon Shire Horse Centre, Yealmpton, Plymouth, Devon.
Steam and Countryside Museum, Sand Bay, Exmouth, Devon.
Dorset Heavy Horse Centre, Edmondsham, Verwood, Dorset.

Spinney Farm, Windmill Hill,
Herstmonceux, East Sussex.
Sussex Shires, Haremere Hall,
Etchingham, East Sussex.
Snowhill Manor, near Broadway,
Gloucestershire.
The Science Museum, Exhibition Road,
South Kensington, London SW7 (01-598
6371).
Rochdale Museum, Sparrow Hill,
Rochdale, Greater Manchester (*Rochdale*
47474 ext 769).
Breamore Countryside Museum, Breamore
House, Breamore, Hampshire
(*Breamore 468*).
Hereford and Worcester County
Museum, Hartlebury Castle, near
Kidderminster, Hereford and
Worcester (*Hartlebury 416*).
Country Centre, Clows Top,
Kidderminster, Hereford and
Worcester (*Clows Top 358*).
Manx Open Air Museum, Cregneash,
Isle of Man (*Douglas 5522*).
Whitbread Hop Farm, Beltring, Paddock
Wood, Kent.
Rutland County Museum, Catmos
Street, Oakham, Leicestershire,
·(*Oakham 3654*).
Museum of Lincolnshire Life, Burton
Road, Lincoln, Lincolnshire (*Lincoln*
28488).
Norfolk Shire Horse Centre, West
Runton, Cromer, Norfolk.
Hasholme Carr Farm, Holme upon
Spalding Moor, York, North Yorkshire.
Staintondale Shires, Eastside Farm,
Staintondale, Scarborough, North
Yorkshire.
Ryedale Folk Museum, Hutton-le-Hole,
North Yorkshire, (*Lastingham 367*).

The King William, Ipsden, Oxfordshire
(*Checkendon 680675*).
Salop County Museum Service,
Wenlock Edge, Acton Scott, Church
Stretton, Salop (*Marshbrook 322*).
Heavy Horse Centre, Cricket St Thomas
Park, Chard, Somerset.
Bass Brewing, Burton on Trent,
Staffordshire.
Easton Farm Park, Easton
Woodbridge, Suffolk.
Museum of East Anglian Life, Abbots
Hall, Stowmarket, Suffolk (*Stowmarket*
2299).
Horsham Museum, Causeway House,
The Causeway, Horsham, West Sussex
(*Horsham 4959*).
Weald and Downland Open Air
Museum, Singleton, near Chichester,
West Sussex (*Singleton 348*).
Pennine Farm Museum, Ripponden,
near Halifax, West Yorkshire (*Elland*
2540).
Welsh Folk Museum, St Fagans, near
Cardiff (*Cardiff 561357*).
Rural Crafts Museum, Llanvapley, near
Abergavenny, Gwent. (*Llantilio 210*)
Brecknock Museum, Brecon, Powys
(*Brecon 4121*).
Adamston Agricultural Museum,
Adamston Farm, Drumblade, near
Huntly, Aberdeenshire (*Drumblade*
231).
Angus Folk Museum, Kirk Wynd,
Glamis, Angus, Tayside.
Ulster Folk and Transport Museum,
Cultra Manor, Holywood, County Down
(*Holywood 5411*).

Glossary

Apron Garment worn by all drivers of turn-outs.

Bevelled shoe Slopes outwards, to make the foot appear bigger.

Blaze White marking down front of face; a lot of white is known as 'bald-headed' in the USA.

Breast Curved part of the plough that turns the furrow.

Breed class Shown to breed standards, without harness or vehicle (see 'in-hand').

By Designates sire.

Cart Two-wheeled vehicle with shafts.

Castrate Make incapable of breeding (male).

Clean legged Free of long hair or feather on lower legs; Percherons and Suffolks are clean-legged breeds.

Clover Forage legume of particular value to horses; can be made into hay.

Coachman Driver of a vehicle with two or more horses.

Collecting ring Adjacent to the showing ring, where exhibits meet just before entry.

Colt Young male horse, uncastrated.

Decorated class Class where the harness and its decorations are of more consequence than the horse itself.

Draught Drawing or pulling. Also 'draft' (USA).

Dray Four-wheeled vehicle with seat; brewers' vehicles are usually termed drays.

Driver Person in charge of a single horse and vehicle.

Dynamometer Device for recording the pull of a horse team, without the team moving a stoneboat.

Entire Stallion.

Felloes, fellies Wooden section of the circumference of the iron-tyred wheel.

Filly Young female horse, usually used in conjunction with age definition eg filly foal.

Finish In ploughing, the place where the furrows meet from opposite directions.

Furrow horse Off-side horse, the right-hand one from the plough stilts;

some furrow horses are trained to walk just clear of the furrow, but retain the name.

Furrow wheel Large wheel that runs in the bottom of the furrow, adjustable for width and depth.

Gelding Castrated male.

Groom In the show world, the assistant in charge of a horse, or the assistant to the coachman, riding with the vehicle.

Handles Part of the plough held by the ploughman.

Headland The end of the furrows, where the teams turn.

High-cut Unbroken furrow set on edge.

Hub caps, cups Caps which screw into the wheel centre and are packed with grease.

In-hand Synonomous with 'breed class'; a single animal shown, usually under breed society standards.

Land horse Near-side horse; the left-hand one from the plough stilts.

Landside Flat part of the plough that presses against the furrow wall.

Land wheel Small wheel that runs on the unploughed ground, adjustable.

Mare Female from three years onwards.

Martingale Leather strap on horse's chest, much used for decoration.

Mouldboard That part of the plough that turns the furrow over (see 'breast').

Naff, nave Hub of a wooden wheel.

Obstacle test A race against time by turn-outs through a series of markers.

Open bridle One without blinkers or blinders, so the horses see can what is behind them; those favouring the open bridle believe that the horse is less nervous when he can see the reason for any noise.

Out of Designates dam.

Plough body See 'breast'.

Point, sock, share Detachable metal point that leads the plough body into the ground. It makes the horizontal cut. Plough points became rather a fetish among ploughmen and before 1939 an incredible range was manufactured. These were standardised to three during World War 2 and no one was worse off.

Pulling contest One or two horses pulling a loaded sledge over a certain distance, the winner continuing to do so when others have failed; the pull may also be recorded on a 'dynamometer'.

Red ticket First prize.

Ring Area in which animals are shown.

Rulley Four-wheeled flat-topped vehicle, usually with shafts for one horse but no seat.

Seedbed Fine, worked-down soil into which seed is drilled.

Shank Rope attached to a halter's headpiece.

Sledge, stoneboat Wheelless transport used in pulling matches, of a known weight and loaded with blocks whose weights are also known.

Stallion Male horse capable of breeding.

Steward Judge's assistant, there to carry out his wishes and facilitate his task.

Stretcher Light wooden pole to keep apart two trace chains when a second horse is hitched to a cart.

Swingle tree Piece of wood or metal with hooks, joining trace chains and implement and holding the chains apart so that they do not chafe the horses' legs.

Temperament Natural disposition eg fiery or placid.

Trade turn-out Normally applies to horses and vehicles used for deliveries or city work, not farm vehicles.

Turn-out Vehicle plus horse(s) in a show class; this is usually for single horse, pair, then three or four or more.

Waggon Four-wheeled farm vehicle whose style varies according to county of origin.

Wagon American version of above; also used to denote a motor vehicle.

Bibliography

Anderson, G.M. *From the Glens to the Lowlands*, New
   Horizon, 1979.
Arnold, James. *The Farm Waggons of England & Wales*,
   David & Charles, 1979.
—*All Drawn by Horses*, David & Charles, 1979.
Baird, Eric. *The Clydesdale Horse*, Batsford, 1982.
Carr, Samuel. *The Poetry of Horses*, Batsford, 1981.
Chivers, Keith. *The Shire Horse*, J.A. Allen, 1977,
   and Futura (abridged), 1978.
— *The London Harness Horse Parade: A Centenary History*,
   J.A. Allen, 1985.
Chivers and Rayner. *The Heavy Horse Manual*,
   David & Charles, 1981.
Cobbett, William. *Rural Rides*, Penguin Books, 1967.
   (First published in 1830.)
Cockcroft, Barry. *Princes of the Plough*, Dent, 1977.
Cummings, Primrose. *The Great Horses*, Dent, 1946.
Day, Herbert. *Horses on the Farm*, Hutton Press, 1981.
—*My Life with Horses*, Hutton Press, 1983.
Dent, Anthony. *Donkey*, Harrap, 1972.
—*Cleveland Bay Horses*, J. A. Allen, 1978.
Ernle, Lord. *English Farming Past and Present*, Heinemann, 1968 (sixth
   edition).
Evans, George Ewart. *The Horses in the Furrow*, Faber & Faber, 1960.
—*Ask the Fellows Who Cut the Hay*, Faber & Faber, 1956
—*The Farm and the Village*, Faber & Faber, 1969.
—*The Pattern Under the Plough*, Faber & Faber, 1966.
—*Horse Power and Magic*, Faber & Faber, 1979.
Fussell, G.E. *The Old English Farming Books (1523-1793)* Aberdeen
   Rare Books, 1978.
Gibbs-Smith, Charles H. *The Bayeux Tapestry*, Phaidon, 1973.
Gilbey, Sir Walter Bt. *The Concise History of the Shire Horse*, Spur
   Publications, 1976. (First published in 1899.)

—*Farmstock of Old*, Spur Publications, 1976. (First published in 1910.)

Gladwin, D.D. *The Waterways of Britain*, Batsford, 1976.

Hadfield, Charles. *British Canals*, David & Charles, 1974.

—*The Canals of South & South East England*, David & Charles, 1969.

Hart, Edward. *Shire Horses*, Batsford, 1983.

—*Care and Showing of the Heavy Horse*, Batsford, 1981.

—*Heavy Horses*, Batsford, 1981.

—*Golden Guinea Book of Heavy Horses, Past and Present*, David & Charles, 1976.

—*Pony Trekking*, David & Charles, 1976.

—*Showing Livestock*, David & Charles, 1979.

—*Victorian and Edwardian Farming from Old Photographs*, Batsford, 1981.

—*The Heavy Horse*, Shire Publications, 1979.

Hayes, Captain M. Horace, FRCVS. *Veterinary Notes for Horse Owners*, Stanley Paul, 1974 (sixteenth edition).

Hennell, Thomas. *The Old Farm*, Robinson Publishing, 1984.

Hogg, Garry. *Hammer and Tongs, Blacksmithery Down the Ages*, Hutchinson, 1964.

Holden, Bryan. *The Long Haul*, J. A. Allen, 1985.

Hughes, G.B. *Horse Brasses for the Collector*, Country Life 1964.

Ingram, Arthur. *Horse-Drawn Vehicles since 1760*, Blandford, 1977.

Janovich, Miklos. *They Rode into Europe*, Harrap, 1971.

Jenkins, J.Geraint. *The English Farm Wagon*, David & Charles, 1972.

Keegan, Terry. *The Heavy Horse, Its Harness and Harness Decoration*, Pelham Books, 1973.

Kilpatrick, James. *My Seventy Years with Clydesdales*, Henry Munro Limited, 1949.

Kitchen, Fred. *Brother to the Ox*, Dent, 1940.

—*Life on the Land*, Dent, 1941.

Lee, Charles E. *The Horse Bus as a Vehicle*, London Transport Executive, 1974.

Leighton, Albert C. *Transport and Communication in Early Medieval Europe AD 500-1100*, David & Charles, 1972.

National Federation of Young Farmers' Clubs. *Farm Horses*, Edward Hart Publications, 1981. (First published in 1943.)

Norman, Vesey. *Arms and Armour*, Weidenfeld and Nicolson, 1964.

—*The Medieval Soldier*, Arthur Barker, 1971.

Oaksey, John and Lord Snowdon. *Pride of the Shires*, Hutchinson, 1979.

Partridge, Michael. *Early Agricultural Machinery*, Hugh Evelyn, 1969.

Reffold, Harry. *Pie for Breakfast*, Hutton Press, 1984.

Reid, J. *Evolution of Horse-Drawn Vehicles*.

Robinson, D.H. (editor). *Fream's Elements of Agriculture*, John Murray, 1962 (fourteenth edition).

Runniquist, A. *The Horse in Fact and Fiction*, 1957.

Russell, Valerie *Heavy Horses of the World*, Country Life, 1983.

Smith, D.J. *The Horse on the Cut*, Patrick Stephens, 1981.
—*Collecting and Restoring Horse-Drawn Vehicles*, Patrick Stephens, 1982.
Somerville and Ross. *Experiences of an Irish RM*, Sphere, 1982.
Stubbs, George. *Anatomy of the Horse*, 1776.
Sturt, George. *The Wheelwright's Shop*, Cambridge University Press, 1963. (First published in 1923.)
Summerhays, R.S. *Encyclopaedia for Horsemen*, Frederick Warne, 1970 (fifth edition).
Telleen, M. *Draft Horse Primer*, Rodale Press, 1977.
Thompson, John. *The Wheelwright's Trade*, 1983.
Trench, Charles Chevenix. *A History of Horsemanship*, Longman, 1970.
Trevelyan, G.M. *Illustrated English Social History*, Longmans, Green & Company, 1944.
Vesey-Fitzgerald, Brian (editor). *Book of the Horse*, Nicholas & Watson, 1946.
Vince, John. *Vintage Farm Machines*, Shire Publications, 1978.
Ward, Gordon R. *On Dating Old Horse Shoes*, 1939.
Watson, J.A. Scott and M.E. Hobbs. *Great Farmers*, Faber & Faber, 1951.
Watson, James A.S. and James A. More. *Agriculture, the Science and Practice of British Farming*, Oliver and Boyd, 1945.
Weatherley, Lee. *Great Horses of Britain*, Saiga, 1978.
—*Heavy Horse Handbook*, Southern Counties Heavy Horse Association, 1972.
Weber and Jepsen, *Heroes in Harness*, A.S. Barnes, 1979.
Whitlock, R. *Gentle Giants*, Lutterworth, 1976.
Wright, Philip A. *Old Farm Implements*, David & Charles, 1974.
—*Salute the Carthorse*, Ian Allan, 1971.
British Percheron Horse Society Stud Books.
Clydesdale Horse Society Stud Books.
The 'Colony' Suffolks, HMSO, 1975.
Shire Horse Society Stud Books.
Suffolk Horse Society Stud Books.

Index